Preceding double page: The Atherton Tablelands, a green plateau landscape of gentle hills west of Cairns, is one of the most fertile regions of Queensland.

"Uluru" means "shady place" in the language of the Anangu aboriginal people. Ayers Rock, the Australian landmark, dominates the expanse of the outback with its height of 348 meters. In the background: the "Olgas".

AUSTRALIA

CONTINENT OF CONTRASTS

Photography   Oliver Bolch
Texts   Roland F. Karl, Jörg Berghoff, Jochen Müssig

Exposed to the elements. In Port Campbell National Park the sea and the winds have shaped the coastline over thousands of years. London Bridge, a rock formation near the coast, collapsed in 1990. A few tourists, who had walked to the end of this natural bridge just shortly before it caved in, had to be rescued by helicopter.

CONTENTS

Marine paradise: on the Great Barrier Reef the clown fish hides amongst the tentacles of the sea anemone if it senses danger. You should not only admire the Whitsunday archipelago from the air. Let your holiday dreams come true by spending some time on these lovely beaches (above and right).

Following double page: The glow of the metropolis of Sydney. Panoramic view from Kirribilli Point: the Opera House, Sydney Cove and Circular Quay with the harbor port area "The Rocks" and the high rise office buildings of the business center behind.

Australia is a huge "playground" for Mother Nature. The lushness and beauty of the natural environment of this continent is unbelievable. One of the many gorgeous spots is Triplet Falls in the Otway State Forest in Victoria.

TAKE IT EASY

The motto of "down under" is "take it easy". This motto applies everywhere – to Scarborough Beach in Western Australia (left), sitting under a boab tree in the Kimberleys (center) and to the driver of this huge road train (right).

Australia has as many impressions in store for its visitors as it has sand on its beaches and in its deserts. A huge amount! Australia's coastline has a total length of 37,000 kilometers (approx. 23,000 miles). It has the largest sand island in the world and boasts no less than four deserts. As a consequence, you need to be equipped with a lot of energy and a good sense for adventure if you want to gather as many impressions as possible during your visit to this "fifth" continent.

"Which place in the world has the most sand?" Ranger Scott Toohey tests us with a grin. Our prompt answer is: "The Sahara of course!" Scottie corrects us: "No, guessed wrong! But don't worry: everyone guesses wrong."

In fact only 10 percent of the surface of the largest desert in the world is covered by sand. Fraser Island in the south of the Australian state of Queensland, around 300 kilometers (186 miles) north of Brisbane, on the other hand, consists entirely of these small grains. Here you can admire a total of seventy-two different colors of sand. The few islanders who live on Fraser are proud of the fact that they not only live on the largest sand island in the world, but also have the largest heap of sand – worldwide. This was reason enough for UNESCO, the special commission of the United Nations in charge of science and culture, to declare the island a natural World Heritage Site.

Australia is not only a country with enormous expanses, but a country of superlatives as well, particularly with respect to spectacular natural features. UNESCO has declared fifteen sites of natural or cultural world heritage on this "fifth continent". Only eleven nations on earth have received more of these nominations, which are most honorable, but also carry certain obligations. The fifteen Australian UNESCO sites illustrate a perfect cross-section

of the bountiful and diverse natural environment of this country.

The dimensions of this southern continent are unusual, too. Although the American continent is around seven times as large as Australia, which has a total area of almost 7.7 million square kilometers (approx. three million square miles), Australia has a presentable maximum width of 4,500 kilometers (approx. 2,800 miles). This is the approximate distance between San Francisco and Washington. And so it comes as no surprise that the largest construction in the world (if you can call it that) is found down under. The Dog Fence has a length of 9,600 kilometers (5,965 miles) and runs from Surfers Paradise in Queensland to the tree-less Nullarbor Plain on the border of South and Western Australia. For the sake of comparison – the Great Wall of China is only about a quarter as long. But then the Great Wall had to be built solidly to withstand the attack of the nomads, whilst the dog fence was merely erected to protect the sheep in the south from the dingoes of the north. It does so quite successfully to this day. Australia is the largest island in the world and the smallest continent at the same time. This sixth largest country on Earth introduced the first national park in 1879 with the Royal National Park, south of Sydney. Now, at the beginning of the 21st century, it prides itself on its more than 500 national parks and its additional 1,500 other nature conservation areas, plus the aforementioned world heritage sites. The spectrum of sites that have been declared as worthy of special protection by UNESCO ranges from

Galvin Gorge in the Kimberleys is an oasis in the middle of no-man's-land (left page). – May I introduce myself, I am a kangaroo (above).

the tropical Kakadu National Park and Purnululu National Park in the north, with its Bungle Bungle rock formations which look like beehives, to the world-famous Great Barrier Reef off the coast of Queensland in the east and the similarly famous Ayers Rock in the center of the Uluru Kata Tjuta National Park in the heart of the country, right down to the Tasmanian wilderness in the south. Three of the islands, or island groups, which have received nom-

"Kangaroos crossing": wherever you see this sign, you should drive slowly. It is a good idea to equip your car with mighty "roo bars", just like those mounted on the car of these farmers on Exmouth Peninsula in Western Australia (below).

inations by UNESCO, extend even further south, right down to Antarctica: Macquaire Island, 1,500 kilometers (900 miles) south of Tasmania, along with Heard Island and the McDonald Islands are Australia's most distant outposts in the Antarctic south of the Indian Ocean. The world heritage sites also include South Pacific regions – with the Lord Howe Island group. Here pointy mountains reach into the sky and turquoise water laps around the island coastline 700 kilometers (435 miles) from Sydney. Fearful sounding, but harmless Shark Bay in the westernmost part of the country belongs to the same noble selection, just like the rainforests of the Central Eastern Rainforest Reserves and the Wet

Tropics of Queensland, as well as the Blue Mountains with their eucalyptus forests, which are responsible for emitting the blue mist which gives these mountains their name. The Blue Mountains are the favorite weekend destination for people who live in Sydney. The Fossil Mammal Sites near Riversleigh in West Queensland which date back to the ice age and the Willandra Lakes Region in the south complete the Australian heritage for mankind. Number ten, Fraser Island, is a good example of the fact that there is always something unexpected waiting for you. Much, much more is usually hidden behind an impressive front, just waiting for you to discover it …

Fraser is like a microcosm. Just like the great mother island, this island is full of surprises. For instance the main rainforest on Fraser is the only one on Earth that thrives on sand. Four and a half million liters of water gush forth daily from a single spring, Eli Creek. This is about the average usage of drinking water for the whole of Sydney. The island is decorated with shifting sand dunes which are more than 200 meters (656 feet) high and up to

"The jeep drivers can see and hear a plane coming. And the pilot has to keep his eyes open, too. But there is easily enough room for both," Ranger Scottie tells us matter of factly.

That's how simple and different life is on Fraser Island. And that's how varied Australia is – a country where you can surf and ski, where camel meat is grilled and crocodile, kangaroo and emu are eaten, but where you can also find the finest haute cuisine. Using

30,000 years old. It boasts forty inland lakes which guarantee a lovely bathing experience with their temperature of around 30 degrees centigrade. It has the famous Eastern Beach which runs along the east coast with a length of at least 100 kilometers (62 miles). In the coastal waters along this beach you will find the highest density of sharks in Queensland. The beach itself supports the longest sand and beach highway, without any road markings, but with a speed limit of 80 kilometers (50 miles) per hour. This speed limit, however, does not apply to the propeller planes which use the beach highway as a runway. Nobody bothers blocking off the highway when aircrafts take-off and land.

Every contact with humans is stressful for koalas. But in the koala hospital in Port Macquarie contact is sometimes inevitable (left).

The owners of the Mungerannie Hotel calmly await new guests (above).

Bumping across the grassy plains of the Gunbarrel Highway in a jeep will give you the proper Australia feel, combined with the pleasure of adventurous driving (above). Road train drivers and tourists alike enjoy a cold beer in the earthy "Birdsville Pub".

the example of Fraser Island, if you only see the sand, you will miss out on a lot. And Fraser is only one of a total of 900 very different islands which are clustered along the 2,000-kilometer (1240-mile) length of the Great Barrier Reef.

In the 90's, new hotel resorts, trendy wellness worlds and a broad

Where the past and the present, tradition and modern times meet: a replica of the legendary "Bounty" anchoring in front of the backdrop of the world-famous Sydney Opera House.

offer of holiday activities were important factors for holiday planning. Today the issue of safety has become prime. Australia is one of the safest holiday destinations. Terrorism is not an issue down under. The smallest continent with the lowest population density is only the fifth wheel in world politics. The government of its capital Canberra only attracts attention politically when it supports Australia's immigration policy which has become extremely rigid.

The former society of immigrants now wants to stay on its own. Some 95 percent of Australians are of European descent, but their roots are not as strong as they used to be. There is no doubt that now in the 21st century Australia has clearly found its political, economic and social environment in the Asia-Pacific region.

Australia wants to keep its country, its enormous deposits of raw materials and the beauty of its natural environment to itself and no longer wants to share it with new arrivals. Of course visitors are warmly welcomed to admire the natural beauty. Around five million tourists from all over the world arrive in Australia each year. But the expanse and size of the country is not enough reason to allow more people to settle in this country permanently. They would only settle in the same places where the majority live already: in the cities and along the east coast. Already now around 50 percent of the almost twenty million Australians, who descend from more than 120 different countries, live in Sydney, Melbourne and Brisbane. The widely quoted population density of around two persons per square kilometer is, at most, of statistical value.

America's population density is fifteen times as high. But when you arrive in Sydney or in Melbourne or even in Perth or Darwin you won't notice this amongst the hectic activity and busy traffic. But still, you will immediately notice that something is different. It is the Australian attitude to life, their way of dealing with things. Workaholics are rare and you will come across very few know-it-alls. And the friendliness is unbeatable. You talk about surfing and not about statistics. The job is a necessity to earn money, but it is not the fulfillment of life. The admirable thing about Australia and its inhabitants – whether they are descendants of stubborn Germans, hard-drinking Irish or cheerful Italians – is the ease and freedom with which they live in a country on the "sunny side of life".

Let's take a typical Sydneysider: young, sporty, handsome, with a great job and even greater opportunities to enjoy his leisure time. Any tourist visiting Sydney for the first time will rave about this city!

See page 26

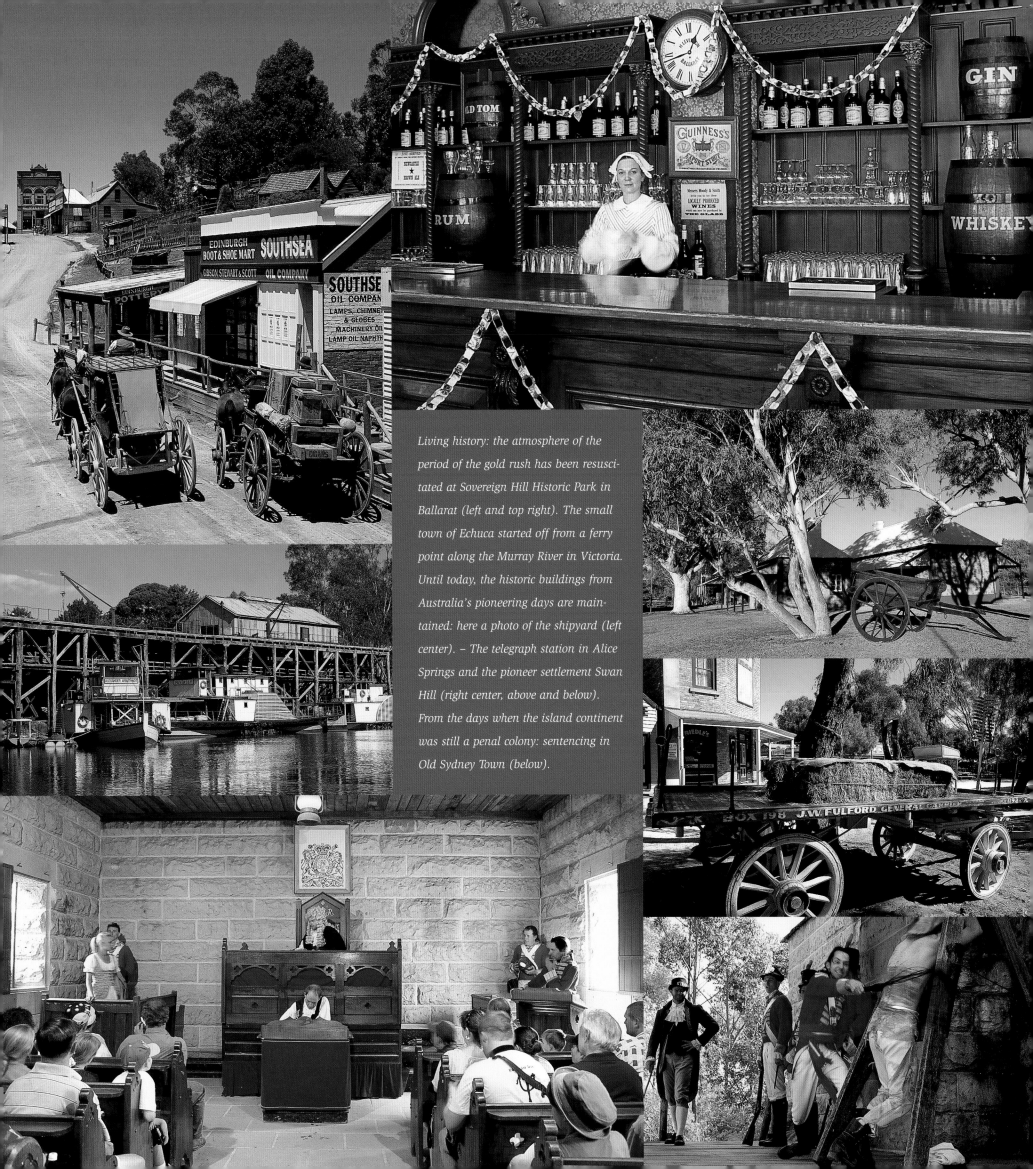

Living history: the atmosphere of the period of the gold rush has been resuscitated at Sovereign Hill Historic Park in Ballarat (left and top right). The small town of Echuca started off from a ferry point along the Murray River in Victoria. Until today, the historic buildings from Australia's pioneering days are maintained: here a photo of the shipyard (left center). – The telegraph station in Alice Springs and the pioneer settlement Swan Hill (right center, above and below). From the days when the island continent was still a penal colony: sentencing in Old Sydney Town (below).

AUSTRALIA'S HISTORY

The first Aborigines colonized Australia around 50,000 years ago. They came across from New Guinea via a land bridge. In 1606, the Spaniard Luis des Torres crossed the strait between New Guinea and Australia. In memory of him it is now called the Torres Strait.

In 1616, the Dutchman Dirk Hartog was probably the first European to set foot on Australian territory: the "Eendracht" sailed to an island

Flinders aboard the "Norfolk" (1789) and William Bligh aboard his legendary mutiny ship, the "Bounty", were not the only ones in the race for Terra Australis Incognita, hoping for fame and fortune. James Cook was the most famous seafarer of them all. Under orders from His Majesty King George III, he sailed around New Zealand on his first trip around the world. On April 30, 1770 he sailed the

1

3

off Australia's west coast which has carried the name Dirk Hartog Island since. In 1642, the Dutchman Abel Janszoon Tasman sailed to what is Tasmania today. The reports of William Dampier, who landed on Melville Island in the northwest in 1688, sounded truly adventurous: he noted Aboriginals who seemed like monsters and a sad, worthless country.

In the 18th century, the discovery of the oceans was organized professionally: the prospering scientific community sent botanists, geologists, writers and painters to join expeditions by ship, which were financed by European governments. Seafarers such as Tobias Furneaux aboard the "Adventure" (1773), Matthew

"Endeavour" into Botany Bay south of Sydney. From there he traveled up the east coast of New Holland and ran aground on the Great Barrier Reef near Cooktown. After the repairs to his "Endeavour" had been completed, he flew the British flag on Possession Island, an island off Cape York, and took possession of the entire eastern part of the continent in the name of the Crown. At this stage the continent was still called New Holland due to the first Dutch seafarers that had arrived there. Following that, Captain Arthur Phillip brought the first prisoners to the island. In early capitalist England it was often enough of a crime to merely steal a loaf of bread to be banished to

Australia. In 1788, eighteen years after Cook's return, Phillip was in command of a fleet of eleven ships with 736 prisoners and just as many civilians on board, 192 women amongst them. The fleet arrived in the Bay of Sydney. The German Philipp Schäffer arrived two years later as a supervisor for the newly established penal colony and was one of the first Germans who were given land for agriculture. There were quite a few Germans amongst the many settlers who poured into Australia. Amongst them was a certain Johann Christoff Pabst who brought seven hundred sheep into the country with the help of four other shepherds. In 1838 Gossner missionaries arrived in Moreton Bay

5

6

populated areas of Australia's north came under Federal administration as the so-called Northern Territory. Initially the Federal Government resided in Melbourne. Then, in 1927, Canberra became its new seat. In both World Wars I and II, the Australians fought on the side of the Allies. In 1962 and in 2000 the Olympic Games were held in Melbourne and Sydney respectively.

To this day, the form of government in Australia – the parliamentary democratic monarchy – remains controversial. Following the outcome of the referendum in 1999, Queen Elisabeth II of England continues to be the official Head of State.

1 Mutiny on the Bounty, painting by Robert Dodd (1748-1816). – 2 James Cook, painting by Nathaniel Dance (1735-1811). – 3 Canberra's ultra-modern New Parliament House. – 4 Sir William Matthew Flinders, British archaeologist (1853-1942) with finds. – 5 Aborigines with didgeridoos. – 6 Australia's Prime Minister John Howard, 2004.

near Brisbane to convert the Aborigines there to Christianity. Hired by Australian farmers, winegrowers from the German Rheingau region established vineyards. When the gold rush broke out in the mid-19th century, after the first nuggets had been found, fortune seekers from all over the world flooded into the country. A further turning point was the construction of the Overland Telegraph Line in 1872 which connected this remote island directly with England. Soon the independent colonies of New South Wales, Tasmania, Western Australia, South Australia, Victoria and Queensland were founded. On January 1, 1901 they united to form the Commonwealth of Australia. The huge, sparsely

23

It is as charming as San Francisco or Rome, has a similarly stunning setting to Rio de Janeiro and Hong Kong and offers almost as much culture as New York, certainly as much as Berlin. The Sydneysider is proud of his city. And the matter of fact way with which he might be studying the waves at Dee Why Beach with a surfboard under his arm, even during the week, tends to really fluster the common European who is used to being harassed by the check clock.

Throughout the 19th and the 20th century Australia was a popular destination for emigrants. Large sailing ships found their way to sheltered bays (left) and into the new heart of the country, Circular Quay in Sydney (below).

Without any doubt Sydney is the center and heart of the country, despite Canberra, the official capital, despite Melbourne, the number two which is intent on catching up and maybe overtaking Sydney. In Sydney life pulsates and trends are set. This is the place where Australia presents itself to the world and not only since the Olympic Games in 2000.

This city of four million has more attractions than all the other Australian cities: an impressive skyline, a huge, natural harbor with hundreds of bays where not only dinghies, yachts and cruise liners sail, but where you can find approximately 750 species of fish. The harbor is crossed by the famous Harbour Bridge, is adorned by the even more famous Opera House and guarded by the TV tower which is more than 300 meters (985 feet) high. At its feet glass palaces rub shoulders with Victorian buildings, and the brick warehouses of the part of town called The Rocks lie adjacent to Darling Harbour with its monorail.

Any visitor can experience a similar excitement, but of a completely different kind, around 1,500 kilometers (approx. 930 miles) northwest of the city: at Ayers Rock, the world-famous symbol of the 40,000 year old culture of the Aborigines. The white Australians know all about their culture, they respect it and market it, but what they often lack is respect for the Aborigines of today. Yes, sure, many live off social security, many are alcoholics, many look ragged. But that is only because the white man took the land away from the black man and thus took away his old culture and roots, too. Each tribe has its territory whose borders were precisely sung about in songs: rock formations, water courses or other significant natural features formed the so-called "lines". An example of the disrespect for the Aborigines is that they were only

tor to Australia. Queensland represents the sunniest side of Australia and offers relaxation and recuperation after the exciting visit to the city and the similarly fascinating and strenuous stay in the desert. Here people lead an outdoor life. This state is a funfair for tourists, sun worshippers and lazybones, for surfers, snorkelers and divers aiming for the Great Barrier Reef, the largest coral reef in the world.

confirmed as rightful owners of Ayers Rock, the second largest monolith in the world, as late as 1985. And bureaucracy is taking its time to return more land to the Aborigines, who only make up 2 percent of the total population, and to let them live there the way they used to for hundreds of years. Sometimes you get the feeling that this can only remain wishful thinking. The urbanization, the partial slums, the ghettoization of the Aborigines has progressed too far, hand in hand with their uprooting and loss of traditions.

The outback with Ayers Rock, Sydney, the gate to the continent, and Queensland are the "musts" for almost every first time visi-

There was a lot of hustle and bustle amongst the new immigrants on Pyrmont Bridge in Sydney, now part of modern Darling Harbour (above), and in the center of town, such as on George Street (left). Previous double page: landscape near Geelong, painting by Eugene von Guerard, 1856.

Even James Cook was amazed at the strange fauna of Australia. The emu and the kangaroo became the heraldic animals of this country. The wombat is known as a cuddly toy for kids. The same cannot be said of the Echidna, a toothless type of hedgehog. The Australian Bustard proudly stalks around in Queensland. The Kookaburra is also called "Laughing Jack" in the Sunshine State. Sooty Terns having a rest, a King Parrot having a look and a few Cape Barren Geese remaining alert (clockwise from top left).

The skipper on the yacht with its snowy white sails welcomes his guests with "G'day mates!" But this is also how the bank apprentice greets the director and the surfer greets the blonde on the beach. The Sunshine State has a laid back attitude, just like Pete, the skipper, who instills fear in his guests in the face of the upcoming snorkel and dive trip on the reef. "You'll see one," he booms, but quickly adds: "No worries! They are the most harmless sharks. The reef sharks which you will see are more afraid of you than you are of them. Consequently they'll swim off quickly and look for easier prey." And of course you might encounter turtles, mantas, clown and surgeon fish and countless other species of fish on a trip to the sheer reef drop-off. Against a backdrop of corals dazzling in all colors and shapes. Cairns, Townsville and Shute Harbour are the three most popular departure points for boat trips to the Great Barrier Reef. Aside from the reef and the beach, funfairs and nightlife, the Sunshine State also has dense rainforest to offer. Leaving Cairns you can take a narrow coastal road north right up to Cape Tribulation National Park. The Daintree National Park starts just outside of Cairns. You can cruise around it comfortably by boat or get a proper ground view of it on foot.

Sydney, as beautiful as it is, is not Australia. The outback and the Aborigines, the Sunshine State Queensland with its outdoor freaks are only part of it, as is the boomerang, the didgeridoo, kangaroos and koalas. But if you get to know the magic triangle Sydney-Ayers Rock-Great Barrier Reef, you'll get a pretty good idea of the diversity of Australia with its three time zones and a coast approximately as long as the Earth's circumference.

The highlights in Australia are extremely varied: modern cities, abandoned mission stations, mighty rainforests, endless expanses of red sand, crocodiles which need to be treated with care, and cuddly koalas. And sometimes the Australian stars can be quite small, only 20 centimeters tall, but dressed to the nines – in tails. We are talking about the Fairy Penguins which have made Philip Island famous, as they have chosen this island which is located less than 100 kilometers (62 miles) south of Melbourne as a breeding site. The event which is commonly referred to as the Penguin Parade takes place at its westernmost tip at The Nobbies. It has become a huge attraction.

The penguins' nests are hidden in the sand dunes. Every evening, as regular as clockwork, they waddle up onto the beach as soon as night falls. Darkness gives them some protection from birds of prey. Then they stop in mid-track for a while and stare at the visitors star-

ing at them. The rangers always set up a few bleachers so that everyone gets a good view of these cute birds. The penguins form a line, one next to the other, so that they can all have a proper look. Any comic strip is dull compared to this … Obviously they then arrive at the same conclusion as every evening: these people are no danger to us. Then they proceed to waddle straight to their nests which can

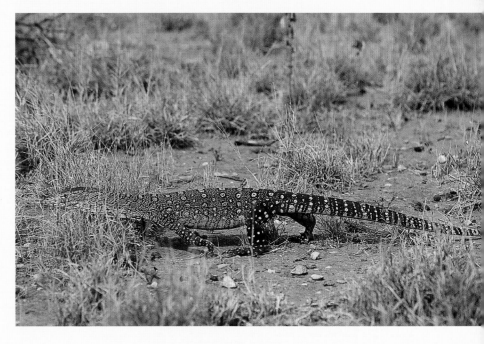

The attraction of every crocodile farm, including Hartley's Creek Farm in Queensland, is feeding time (top). – A Goanna in Western Australia (bottom).

sometimes be up to 50 meters (160 feet) from the sea. They have already forgotten about the spectators. And their chicks are hungry … "Our ship lies in calm waters and is surrounded by sixteen islands: one large one, a medium-sized one and fourteen small ones." It was a lovely Friday morning on June 8, 1770. The name of the ship was

The 500 tribes of Aborigines make up less than 2 percent of Australia's population. Nevertheless, their culture has survived, such as in the Tjapukai Cultural Park in Cairns where an Aborigine demonstrates the technique of spear-throwing.

"Endeavour" and the quoted log book entry was made by Captain James Cook. Although he did not discover Australia, he explored particularly the east coast like no other.

In 1616, the first white man set foot on Terra Incognita somewhere in the southern hemisphere where explorers had, since the 2nd century, assumed Australia's existence: Dirk Hartog called it New Holland. But as the first landings occurred in the north and then also in the west, one first presumed that it was the poorest country on Earth: as late as 1688 the first Brit merely reported back about the presence of sand, flies, a few animal tracks and natives. Only with James Cook did this image of Terra Incognita gradually change. He landed on the east coast near Sydney on April 30, 1770 and was amazed at how fertile the place was. On his expeditions he also came across the Family Islands on the said day of June 8. His logbook entry noting this event was quoted earlier. The Family Islands lie around 300 kilometers (185 miles) north of Fraser Island. Cook gave them that name as they consist of fourteen small islands grouping around the largest island, "The Father" and the next largest island, "The Mother" – much like chicks huddling around the cockerel and the hen.

Our dinghy has eight horsepower and creates an uplifting "Endeavour" feeling. It enables us to discover the region of the Family Islands, whose tourism is managed by David and Caroline Henry. Each day we can visit another one of the fourteen small, unpopulated baby islands. The Father is now called Dunk Island and the Mother is called Bedarra. The resort on Bedarra is one of the most tranquil and beautiful resorts in the world. If Dunk is the island for those rich in children, then Bedarra can rightly claim to be the island for rich children. And if you happen to find Bedarra too crowded at any time (a maximum of 30 guests share the entire place …), you can ask the staff to prepare a small motor boat for you for a tour around the island. Apart from an island chart, towels, snorkel and mask you will also find a deliciously packed picnic basket in your boat, which can be easily steered without a driver's license or any prior experience. The trip to the twin islands Toolghar and Coomboo takes a good hour. No resort, no people, just a lot of sun, sand, beach, palm trees, daydreams, peace and the gourmet picnic: wine and champagne – chilled of course – chicken and lobster, cheese and crackers, antipasti and everything else that belongs to a sumptuous little feast. The chef packs the picnic basket so generously that any Robinson on any island could also invite a Friday to join him … The motto is: living like God in Australia.

One of the most fascinating landscapes is that of the Bungle Bungles in Western Australia. The rocky mounds look much like beehives (left). – Some of the Aboriginal rock paintings at Nourlangie Rock in Kakadu National Park are claimed to be more than 20,000 years old (above).

Following double page: Knox Gorge is one of the spectacular canyons of the Hamersley Range. Near Karijini National Park, where Knox Gorge is located, geologists came across the oldest mainland on Earth.

FOOD IS SERVED!

EXCELLENT WINE AND MULTICULTURAL CUISINE

The horror starts in the morning. While everywhere else in the world people gently wake up their palate with fresh rolls, warm croissants straight from the oven or crunchy slices of toast, the Australians come straight to the point. After all the body needs to get going. And what could be better than a good, whole-

thing that was not too successful was its international marketing. It is an acquired taste, but it is worth giving it just one try. Decide for yourself whether this is the start of a great culinary love affair. Be prepared for surprises, Australian cuisine has many of them in store for you. Fortunately the former Anglo-Saxon influ-

some lubricant? The magic mixture which is part of any breakfast in Australia, just as much as the rising sun, is black and sticky with a unique smell. It is the famous Vegemite.

This creamy paste made of vegetable, yeast and malt extracts must be highly addictive. The Australians devour tons of it every year and have little sympathy if you do not like the stuff, as it is part of their national identity. There are two ways of "enjoying" it: spread thinly on buttered toast, or dabbed onto sausages and cheese to spice things up. Songs and poems have been dedicated to it; the only

ences on kitchen and cellar have meanwhile completely faded into the background. Primarily the immigrants from Asia and Southern Europe breathed some life into the frequently boring, overcooked food by using spices and creating crunchy salads. They introduced dressings, hitherto unknown, and created the basis for the strength and special characteristic of Australian cuisine: an unsurpassable diversity of fresh products, ranging from vegetables over meat, seafood and game to fruit and drinks which are certainly no longer limited to icy cold beers. Particularly in the cities, but

In the Barossa Valley, wines are tasted in tasting cellars, such as Angaston (left), on wine estates, such as Chateau Dorien (above) and in family-operated vineyards, such as Pirramimma. Here you can rely on the trusted advice of Alex Johnston while looking out over the vineyards (right).

also in rural areas, Australian chefs create true culinary miracles. And it is noticeable how many female chefs there are amongst them, such as Darilyn Goldsmith of Goldsmiths in the Forest in Lakes Entrance who tells me: "A picnic of fresh seafood, sweet local peaches and fresh cheese, followed by fantastic chocolates. And maybe a crisp Chardonnay to wash it all down. Authentic, fresh, seasonal products and natural herbs and spices is the recipe behind the new Australian food philosophy." That is the whole secret behind the revolution of Australian cuisine, a cuisine which has man-

aged to acquire an excellent reputation – internationally. Whether it be goat's cheese from Western Australia, cold pressed olive oil from the south or Tasmanian salmon – in this country food turns into a sensual feast.

On top of that there is this irresistible culinary pioneer spirit. Bush tucker is one of the most dominant trends in Australia. Traditional dishes such as steak 'n' eggs, meat pie with tomato sauce or roasted lamb have been replaced by tender kangaroo, filets of emu and crocodile, which tastes a little like chicken. If you are in a hurry, a simple portion of fish 'n' chips can be okay. But true culinary discoveries include species of fish such as shark and barramundi from the north or the Sydney Rock oysters. In gourmet gastronomy as well as in Chinese, Greek, Indian, Italian, Japanese or Vietnamese restaurants you will come across more and more special dishes which are strongly influenced by the outback. There is no limit to the multitude of herbs, vegetables, reptiles and insects from the Australian bush which are unfamiliar to our palate. Snake, possum meat and witchetty grubs – which taste a little like almonds – beetles, bush tomatoes, lemon myrtle, the Kakadu plum or fat-free bunya-bunya nuts now appear on the menus. The exotic ingredients of bush tucker or bush food are not only healthy, but taste so good that you feel like trying every single one of the

culinary outback variations. Unless there is a barbie luring. No, that is not an Australian beauty queen, but a barbecue – part of the Australian lifestyle. And if you happen to come across the photo model Jennifer Hawkins at such a barbie, you can guess what she missed most in the run-up to the Miss Universe 2004 elections in Quito: Vegemite of course. She is living proof that this spread is not only incredibly healthy, but ensures timeless beauty, too.

The positive changes in Australian cuisine have also influenced the variety of beverages available. The Australians now drink tea, coffee in every variation or fresh juices, although it must be said that they still are primarily beer drinkers. Although beer consumption has reduced slightly in the past few years, on average around 90 liters are still guzzled per person per year. People living in the hot north enjoy

even more and come close to the Bavarians – they drink around twice as much as their fellow citizens elsewhere. They enjoy their beer icy cold out of cans, bottles or freshly drawn in the pub. The quality of Australian beer is consistently good. The various brews are usually light and zesty and pleasant to drink. Over 120 breweries and more and more smaller pub breweries fight for a share of the market. It is well known that cans have many more uses than just to be cracked open. They serve as a unit of measurement, too, to determine distances. You should

be prepared for this when traveling in the interior. The answer to your question of how far it is to Broken Hill could well be "six cans" in a

Whether it is fish, game, poultry or meat, whatever is served in Australia's restaurants is usually of excellent quality. – Robert's Restaurant at Pepper Tree vineyard in the Hunter Valley has a stylish atmosphere (above). – Sydney's oysters which come straight from the fish market are famous (above right). – Picnic and barbecues in Jervis Bay are popular with gourmets and with surfers (left).

typical pragmatic Australian way. The beer tradition in this country started in 1794 in Sydney when John Boston first started brewing beer. Shortly after 1886, beer production enjoyed its first peak, when the Foster brothers brewed bottom-fermented beer in Victoria. Aside from Fosters, which has become internationally known, the Australian sense of local patriotism is expressed by preferring the local beer. A Melburnian will insist on his Victoria Bitter, a Queenslander on his Four-X and a Tasmanian will stick to his Cascade or Boag's.

Australia's wine growers have also almost completely stopped the long habit of imitating particularly the European traditions of wine growing and wine storage. Today, Australian wines with their uniqueness, the fact that they are made of pure breeds of grapes and their specific growing conditions not only enrich the culinary creativity in Australia, but worldwide. Meanwhile, they

belong to the best wines on our planet. Proof of this are the prestigious awards they win at international wine fairs, more and more frequently. The art of the winemakers of the Barossa Valley, the Margaret River region, of the Yarra and Hunter Valleys or Tasmania cannot be valued highly enough. They manage to grow world-class wine under sometimes extreme climatic conditions. Around 900 million liters of wine are produced by around 1,000 different wineries. Most vines originally came from France. Today 60 percent of Australian wine that is produced is white, 40 percent is red. The most important whites are Chardonnay and Sémillion, the most important reds are Shiraz, Cabernet-Sauvignon, Pinot Noir and Merlot. Last but not least we would like to mention a German type of vine which is attracting more and more attention. If you have the chance, try the semi-dry Riesling from Tasmania. It has a very special, fruity bouquet.

Surfers are in paradise in Queensland (above). The acacia is a treat for plant lovers (center). The Atherton Tablelands, here a picture of Kuranda Railway Station, attracts romantic souls (bottom). Gorgeous beaches, such as Palm Cove, lure sun worshippers to the Sunshine State (right).

QUEENS-LAND

CAIRNS
GREAT BARRIER REEF
FRASER ISLAND
BRISBANE

Fraser Island, the largest sand island in the world, is part of our world heritage according to a prestigious designation by UNESCO. This island boasts tropical forests, white beaches and forty-two freshwater lakes. Stunning Lake Wabby is one of them.

There are worlds between them: a Crimson Rosella in Lamington National Park, inland from the Gold Coast (left), Rosalind Alderley on Alderley Station (center), children being introduced to a dolphin in "Sea World" (right).

There are countless gorgeous islands, reefs, mountains and endless beaches along the Queensland coast between Surfers Paradise and Cape York. After such a large blast of nature, buzzing Brisbane offers urban reorientation.

The occupation of the "red continent" started with a shipwreck. In 1770 Captain Cook sailed his "Endeavour" up the east coast of New Holland, a name given to Australia by Dutch seafarers at the time, and ran aground on the Great Barrier Reef near Cooktown. Cook freed his ship in no time by throwing a few of the heavy canons overboard and, once on land, he flew the British flag and occupied the entire coast in the name of King George III of England. Cook reported back to Europe that this country offered seemingly endless opportunities. That was the start of the colonization of Australia – and of Queensland. British administration officials, convicts, missionaries and traders followed in the wake of the explorers. The traders in particular were often men without many scruples. There were frequent incidents with the original inhabitants, the Aborigines, who felt that they were being robbed of their land. Between 1870 and 1900 Queensland experienced a gold rush when gold was discovered in Charters Towers and at Palmer River. Right up to the late 70's of the previous century, Australia's legendary east coast attracted immigrants, adventurers and hippies like a magnet. They came from all around the world and after having arrived in one of the large cities in the south, Sydney or Melbourne, they did not waste any time in heading north on the Pacific Highway. Land prices, even with best ocean views, were still ridiculously low and the climate was superb. Townsville, the busy port town in North Queensland, for instance, has an average of 300 sunny days a year. Quickly a white society established itself in this thinly populated country. The way of life was outlined by the magic names of the places. The "Aussies" could enjoy whatever offered itself to them on their Gold, Sugar and Sunshine Coasts in Queensland and it was a question of patriotism to have been to Surfers Paradise. At the time Brisbane only developed very slowly in the center of this sub-tropical wealth. In fact the "real" urbanites in the south mocked this provincial capital. In the vicinity of the city there were countless islands along coasts which looked like something from paradise. There were lonely sandy bays and palm-fringed beaches which were so long that they stretched beyond the horizon. The hinterland with its extensive sugar cane plantations, the gentle landscapes of mountains and hills with sheep and cattle peacefully grazing between romantically located farms formed an appealing contrast to the sandy and sun-spoilt coastal landscape. The total length of the coast between the Gold Coast and Cape York in the extreme north is 3,000 kilometers (1865 miles). And then there is the largest coral reef in the world, The Great Barrier Reef. This is Queensland's natural wonder which attracts millions of visitors every year. It runs parallel to the coast, along a length of about 2,000 kilometers (approx. 1240 miles), and shows its amazing colors above and below water.

Australia's second largest territory has 3.5 million inhabitants, with every third person living in Brisbane. Meanwhile, the subtropical metropolis looks confidently towards Sydney and Melbourne. The times of provincial Sleeping Beauty have been passé since Brisbane hosted the Expo World Exposition in 1988. The

The Millaa Millaa Falls lie hidden in the rainforest of the Atherton Tablelands, not far from Cairns (left page). An Aborigine from North Queensland (above).

Expo started the change of a former surfer and leisure capital to a center of trade and high finance. Skyscrapers and mirrored fronts define the appearance of the city today. There is a lot of glass, chrome and marble. Left-over treasures from colonial times such as Old City Hall, the General Post Office, the splendid Victorian architecture of the Central Railway Station or St. Stephen's Cathedral now look like foreign objects. In Brisbane's pedestrian zone,

Great Sandy National Park on Fraser Island is strictly protected due to its unique natural environment. Eli Creek is a paradise for canoeists and hikers (left).

Queen Street Mall, endless shopping pleasure is to be had in air-conditioned shopping arcades. The former Expo site, too, has become a meeting place where urban life pulsates along an artificial lagoon surrounded by a rainforest scenario, between restaurants and pubs. Of course the capital offers numerous places of entertainment for night owls, but the best place for partying lies beyond the city limits. There where everything once began – in the former little coastal town of Eiston. At the time Eiston had what surfers were looking for: a long, flat beach with a long and powerful surf zone. So the little community of Eiston cleverly decided to change its name to "Surfers Paradise". This was the

start of an incredible tourism boom. Legions of people now traveled to the Gold Coast, whose broad sandy beach extends from Brisbane down to the border to New South Wales. Since then, the Australian equivalent of Miami Beach, which attracts three million visitors per year, has been growing and growing intensely, mainly in height. In this growing heap of buildings, former coastal towns – sleepy beach spots only a few decades ago – have now been amalgamated into the "City of Gold Coast" for administrative purposes. Today you can usually only get a view of the blue Pacific from the top floors of these concrete castles, but only if they are in the front row. This is the way it is "down under":

civilization culminates in one place and only a few Australian miles inland the outback starts. But in any case, such a culmination is a good prerequisite for an exciting night life.

North of Brisbane the more relaxed Sunshine Coast begins. Orange, pineapple, paw-paw and banana plantations, and green sugar cane fields seam a tropical coastal landscape whose lagoons and lakes enthuse anglers and friends of water sports. Driving

Continuing north, the density of sugar cane fields increases. This is where the Sunshine Coast becomes the Sugar Coast before reaching idyllic Maryborough where a ferry takes you across to the largest sand island in the world, Fraser Island. This ecological treasure trove contains huge areas of sand dunes, over forty freshwater lakes, lush, green rainforest and snowy white beaches. These attributes have rendered this island a worthy candidate for

along Bruce Highway, which connects Brisbane with Cairns – a distance of 1,800 kilometers (1,120 miles) – you will spot several attractions as you cruise along, including the bizarre volcanic cones of the Glasshouse Mountains which even amazed Cook when he sailed by at the time. The highway passes a dozen national parks of which there are admirably many in Australia, namely over 500! In the Mooloolaba River National Park, where visitors are guided through an impressive underwater world in glass tunnels without getting wet in "Underwater World", you start to guess what paradise is waiting to be discovered beyond the coast.

"75 Mile Beach" on Fraser Island rises impressively out of the blue of the Pacific. It supports a beach highway (above). – A fisherman casting his net at Cooloolai Creek on Fraser Island. Only in a few of the lakes and rivers of the island are there fish – the clear, pure water is too nutrient-poor (left).

UNESCO's "World Heritage List". Numerous dingoes, wild horses, wallabies and
more than 200 bird species are found here.
Between August and October, even hump-
backs migrate past its northern tip.

What would Queensland be without its
islands? It would still be a dream, but its
islands are truly special. There are
between 600 and 700 of them, stringed
along like pearls on a necklace – from
Fraser to Lizard Island, the northernmost
one. This string of pearls runs parallel to
Bruce Highway in the vast lagoon between
the coast and the reef. The vast majority of
them are uninhabited, only around two
dozen of them have been developed for
tourism. Keith Williams was one of the
busiest developers, pursuing his own economic aims. This Australian businessman,
who enjoyed great success with trained
seals, dolphins and a water ski show in his
"Sea World", wanted to market the
grandiose Great Barrier Reef in a big way
and implemented a huge construction project. He chose Hamilton Island, one of the

seventy-four islands of the Whitsunday archipelago. First he moved two million cubic meters (70 million cubic feet) of earth by pushing two mountains into the sea to build a tarmac runway for large aircraft. Now scheduled aircraft from Sydney, Brisbane and other cities of the mainland can touch down and take off near the reef. Helicopters and twin-engine aircrafts are constantly on standby, as well as seaplanes to take day trippers out to the reef for snorkeling. Despite the tough opposition of conservationists, this 200 million dollar investment created a busy holiday village out of a hitherto unspoiled island paradise. It has its own harbor with berths for hundreds of yachts. There is a smart promenade lined with restaurants, there are super markets, boutiques, discos and even a hospital. Hotels and apartment buildings several stories high have a total of 2,000 beds. Dive and snorkel trips to the nearby reef are organized by helicopters which can drop you off there within thirty minutes. While the helicopters hover on anchored platforms above water, those not so keen to get themselves wet can get

Carnavon Gorge is a sandstone canyon 30 kilometers (19 miles) in length (right). In Carnavon National Park you can admire orchids, ferns and mosses.

chauffeured through this wonderful world of corals in a submarine boat, which the skipper steers closely along the reef drop-off. When, at the end of such a visit to the reef, helicopters and seaplanes take off again, the next shift is already on its way. The next lot of snorkelers lands on the floating platforms, right on schedule. This type of perfect marketing has not affected all of the islands. There are different forms of tourism development, ranging from low-

Kodak Beach has the skyline of Brisbane as a backdrop (very top). The dolphin show at "Sea World" (above) is perfectly choreographed. – View of Surfers Paradise, Australia's Miami Beach (right).

budget camping on Lady Musgrave or Fraser Island to 500-dollar luxury resorts. Brampton Island, 500 kilometers (310 miles) north of Brisbane, can be reached easily by boat or airplane from the pretty sugar cane town Mackay. On your approach you will have a view over a tropical paradise garden of dense, jungle green vegetation in between colorful shimmering reefs and snow white sand banks with hues of turquoise to dark blue, just like a picture postcard. Almost the entire area around Brampton has been designated a national park. Boats transfer divers and snorkelers to the reef or drop off romantic couples, equipped with a picnic basket and icy cold champagne, in lonely bays. Emus, kangaroos and an amazing array of birds complete the picture of "Heavenly Brampton" as the island likes to call itself. A heavenly experience in the midst of this amazing scenery is "Tube Riding". Sitting on what seems to be an oversized car tire, you are dragged behind a motor boat with breathtaking speed. Right through the waves. The spray and the fountains of water make you feel dizzy!

For visitors looking for a more tranquil experience and for whom money is not an object, Bedarra is the place. They can only get there via Dunk Island, one of the most famous reef islands, as Bedarra is so small that it hasn't even got its own runway. Flying up from Townsville is a lovely experience: Magnetic Island, Orpheus Island, the Palm Islands and countless other islets reminiscent of Robinson Crusoe lie between the mountain chains of the coastal mainland and the bright chain of the "Inner Reef" in the middle of the blue South Pacific. Until Captain Cook discovered Dunk Island in 1770, the Aborigines called their tropical island "island of peace and abundance". Today Dunk can still use this label in parts as 75 percent of the island is national park, whose flora creates a typical rainforest atmosphere in which 150 different bird species flutter around. Cows and horses graze peacefully on the higher-lying pastures of a former farm which the holiday resort markets, too, by offering pony riding, cow milking and evenings huddled around the open fireplace. Those who use Dunk merely as a transfer point, quickly make their way from the runway to the pier to catch their boat to Bedarra.

"A club so exclusive, you can't find the members." This is the advertising slogan of this luxury resort, adding that this paradise will most probably never be seen by most visitors to Queensland. The VIP list seems endlessly long. But Fergie and Elton John have definitely hidden away in one of the secluded huts on stilts and have enjoyed the view over the other picturesque islands outlined against the horizon like in a dream.

See page 56

WORLD WONDER UNDER WATER

THE GREAT BARRIER REEF – A NATURAL PARADISE

With its endless reefs, the Great Barrier Reef is one of the natural wonders of our planet. You get the very best view of its awesome dimensions from the window of a plane. Only with this bird's eye view will you

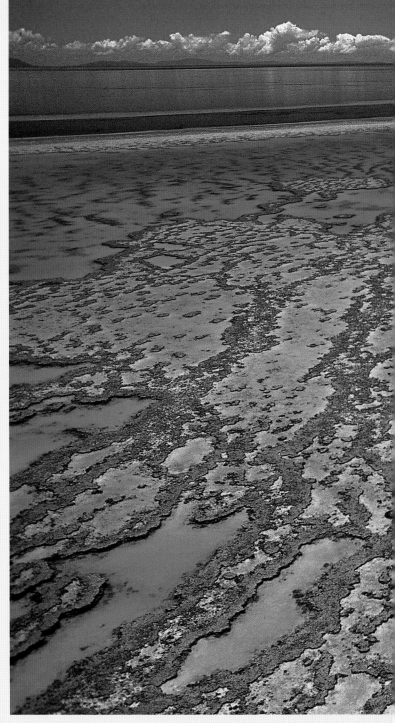

drops into the Pacific Ocean, right down to depths of 2,000 meters (1.2 miles), the play of colors stops and the water turns a uniform deep blue. The Outer Reef is very close to the mainland near Cairns, whereas at Mackay it

see the full splendor of its many hues of blue and turquoise. This natural wonder is 2,000 kilometers (approx. 1250 miles) long, extending from the Tropic of Capricorn south of Rockhampton right up to the coast of Papua New Guinea. Rightfully, the largest and most beautiful reef in the world is being strictly protected and has been placed on the World Heritage List. What lies hidden under water has been made up of 3,500 individual reefs which have grown from the depths over millions of years to display their full colors up in the sun-lit shallower water. Where the Outer Reef steeply

lies over 200 kilometers (125 miles) offshore. In between, in the vast Great Barrier Reef lagoon, the wealth of creation is visible. Broken pieces of coral and sand that has been washed in from elsewhere form islands. Around 300 such coral islands have emerged from the water surface and have turned into magical Robinson Crusoe images, particularly if coconut palm seeds have been blown there, too, and juicy green palm fronds blow in the breeze, thus delivering the loveliest scenery. The elevations of these tiny idylls are rarely higher than a meter above sea level. Currents,

1,500 species of fish, including the clown fish, the parrot fish and other tropical beauties such as the bat fish with its long fins and the colorful pipe fish. And also for sea horses, sea snakes, sea anemones, sea urchins and sea monsters, including the octopus with its long tentacles, squirting cuttlefish and stinging jelly fish. Some of the colorful exotics can be quite dangerous to humans. The lionfish for instance is as poisonous as a cobra. The dreaded stonefish with its grey back and poisonous dorsal spines, which likes to hide amongst dead coral, is also to be avoided. Touching it means risking your life. Snorkelers should also not come too close to moray eels and manta rays, should avoid certain marine snails, which shoot off highly poisonous arrows, and should certainly keep away from the most dreaded creature of all seas, the shark.

Divers and snorkelers arrive at Hardy Reef with boats and seaplanes (left page) to experience the wonderful underwater world including sea dragons (above) and the Coral Banded Shrimp (left). – Hardy Reef seen from above (large photograph).

winds and storms can easily blow them away again. Only continental islands, which used to be part of the mainland at one time, support dense vegetation, such as the lush rainforest on Dunk. There are 600 of them, spread between the coast and the reef. Around 400 different species of coral are the skilled builders of this fragile marine ecosystem. Giant forests of branching corals, the brain corals with their countless convolutions as well as antler, mushroom and plate corals form the basis of the ecosystem of the Coral Sea which explodes with life. They form the basis for

Whitsunday Island is the largest of the seventy-four islands of the Whitsunday archipelago with a total area of 109 square kilometers (42 square miles). There are no hotels on the island, but simply heavenly beaches, such as Whitehaven Beach (left). – Waterfalls, gorges and the Natural Bridge attract visitors to the Springbook National Park south of Brisbane (above).

Lizard Island, which can be reached from Cairns, is another exclusive place. Its attraction is based on the fact that is not even 20 kilometers (12 miles) away from the spectacular dive sites of the "Outer Reef" where the "Cod Hole" is found – one of the five best dive sites in the world. If you swim out just 10 meters from the shore, you will have the living reef straight below you. There is a good reason why a marine research station is present on the island. In its guest book

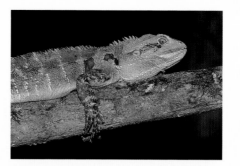

The Daintree National Park near Port Douglas is famous for large and small reptiles (left). The Curtain Fig Tree seems to be a freak of nature. This one was photographed in the Yungaburra Forest, Atherton Tablelands (below).

you will find the names of many well-known marine scientists from all around the world. Visitors relax in the neighboring Lizard Island Lodge which has counted Prince Charles and Tom Cruise amongst their guests. But between August and November there probably would not be a single spare bed left for them, as this is the when the "Lizard Island Black Marlin Classic" is held, the famous big-game fishing competition. The adventurer James Cook was here, too, on August 12, 1770. As he couldn't find his way out through the reef to leave the island, Cook climbed up to the highest point of the island to get a better overview for a possible exit. This point, which is just under 400 meters high, has been called "Cook's Look" ever since.

Cairns has long moved on from being a dreamy coastal town. It has developed into a pulsating tourist center with an international airport catering for large passenger planes from overseas. It calls itself "Gateway to the Wet Tropics". Here, at the edge of the wilderness, contrasts are particularly stark. The world of the Aborigines, which can hardly integrate into the system of a modern society which is influenced by technology, back packers staying in budget accommodation, hungry for the urban scene, yacht owners whose yachts are berthed in the marinas of Cairns and masses of visitors from all around the world who enjoy the snack and gourmet temples of a multi-cultural society of immigrants and who love a freshly tapped icy cold Foster's or Four-X beer, just like the locals.

Whoever arrives here wants to move on: beyond Cairns lies the Cape York Peninsula which has an area of more than 200,000 square kilometers (approx. 77,000 square miles) – double the size of Portugal. In 1988, UNESCO declared this adventurous piece of Australia a natural world heritage site. Inaccessible rainforest dominates the

Beyond Mossman the highway becomes a gravel road which leads through picturesque rainforests and along golden beaches on its way up to Cape Tribulation, which used to be the destination of hippies and back packers from all over the globe. This is where the road ends for most. Only the adventurous with a lot of experience continue the trip on rough four-wheel tracks, which follow the coast of inaccessible rainforest, and head for Cooktown. Then

landscape. Apart from a few Aboriginal reserves, a few settlements and isolated farms, this peninsula is almost uninhabited.

The tarmac of the Captain Cook Highway extends up to the exclusive holiday destination of Port Douglas. There is a lot to see en route: stunning, roaring waterfalls in Mossman Gorge, a wild, romantic, forested canyon. In the Daintree River nearby you can admire the dangerous "Salties", Australia's notorious saltwater crocodiles. These free roaming reptiles are not fenced in, therefore visitors to the area need to take the warning signs on the river banks very seriously. Tragically, people who are not careful enough and are all too bold periodically fall victim to crocodile attacks.

The "Salties", Australia's dreaded saltwater crocodiles, do not mind freshwater and human flesh. These animals can grow up to 6 meters (20 feet) long (above). The Cassowary derives its name from the horn helmet on its head. Cassowaries cannot fly, but can clock up speeds of up to 50 kilometers (30 miles) per hour on foot (left).

it is still an 800-kilometer (500-mile) drive on rough tracks from this former gold diggers town to the tip of the continent, to Cape York. This drive past inaccessible marshes and through dense rainforest is considered one of the last adventures left. But the trip can be made far more comfortable, albeit less adventurous: there are luxurious cruise liners which depart from Cairns and sail up to Thursday Island via Lizard.

Most visitors merely scratch Queensland's surface anyway and only visit its coast where 90 percent of all inhabitants live. But if you have a look at a map, you will see the proper dimension of Queensland. With its almost two million square kilometers (approx. 770,000 square miles) it is as large as Western Europe! Aside from the thousands of miles of lovely beaches, islands and reefs, exploring the hinterland can be a great experience. For instance, you can hop on the Kuranda Railway, a historic train from the 19th century, which departs from Cairns and steams to Kuranda via the Atherton Tablelands, whose highest elevation is 1,000 meters (0.62 miles). On this spectacular panoramic train ride, "one of the world's most scenic railway journeys", you will enjoy a lovely landscape crossed by many rivers. On its fertile slopes rice and tobacco are cultivated and you may spot some of the magnificent giant cedar and kauris which grow here. In the outback, which extends west of the coastal mountain range to the border of the Northern Territory and from the Gulf of Carpentaria in the north right down to South Australia, time has no meaning. In this vast land of savannas and semi-deserts there are few individual farms and in the far west you will come across deserted mines or some that are still in operation, including the largest mine in Australia, Mount Isa. Here, smaller gold and diamond mines are scattered, where fortune hunters still dig around today. What space and time means in the Australian outback is best illustrated by the thousands of kilometers of dirt roads along which the notorious road trains pull long clouds of dirt behind them in the heat of this dry country.

The coral beaches of the Fitzroy Islands, here Nudey Beach, are a paradise for snorkelers and divers. The romantic islands are only a 45-minute boat trip away from Cairns (both photos).

Where sailing dreams become reality: you leave Airlie Beach and Shute Harbour for trips through Queensland's magnificent island worlds. The Whitsunday Islands are considered the most beautiful sailing region in Australia – if not worldwide. Luckily it does not take long to reach them, they can be seen from the mainland. On the charter yacht "Derwent Hunter" the motto is: "Sailors live life to the full". This applies to the daily "work" or to sun bathing and simply enjoying!

*The "Aussies" enjoy the cane
toad races at PK's Jungle Village
on Cape Tribulation (above). –
Pristine nature, roaring waterfalls and clear streams, in
which platypuses still live, can
be found north of Mackay, in
the Eungella National Park
(right).*

*Shute Harbour, view from the
Lookout Coffee Shop
(following double page).*

COAT HANGERS AND CORRUGATED IRON ROOFS

FACETS OF AUSTRALIAN ARCHITECTURE

To Australians, coat hangers are by no means strange objects which they do not need as they spend the whole year on the beach clad merely in a T-shirt. Unless they live in the deepest outback, Australians have a well developed sense for fashion which ranges from casual over futuristic to classic chic. Whether bought in a shop or tailored, in Australia clothes of every description are also kept neatly on clothes hangers. The Australians demonstrate their pragmatic nature by their choice of nicknames for their buildings and attractions. Which other nation would ever think of calling an architectural feat, such as the Harbour Bridge in Sydney, the coat hanger? In 1932, this bridge of iron and steel, whose

shape really does remind you of those useful wire objects which inhabit our wardrobes all around the world, was completed after eight years of construction. It shortened the distance between the city center in the south of the harbor and the residential areas in the north of Sydney by a grand total of 25 kilometers (16 miles). Six million screws, 50,000 tons of steel and twenty million dollars were used to construct this work of art whose details are at least as impressive as the Sydney Opera House. The coat hanger has a total length of 503 meters (1,650 feet) and a total height of 134 meters (440 feet). This steel construction is equipped with eight lanes for cars, two railway tracks and a separate path each for cyclists and for

pedestrians. Since 1992, however, a tunnel which runs beneath the harbor serves to alleviate the traffic. For those who have not yet got enough of a view over the harbor and the city from the viewing platform of the museum,

During the "Sydney Festival" the Opera House and Harbour Bridge are lit up colorfully by night (left). Melbourne's skyline balances height and width (above). Not only the sail roofs of the Sydney Opera House symbolize movement, this sculpture in front of its gates reaches for the sky, too (right).

which is located in one of the two impressive bridge pylons and is 88 meters (334 feet) high, can go higher. You wouldn't be in Australia if the thrill of adventure would not attract you to a courageous, but safe tour to the highest point of the coat hanger. Following a serious talk about safety regulations and strict looks by the guide, you can climb up to the highest arch of the bridge.

The Opera House is the second spectacular construction at Sydney's harbor. Today it is the architectural landmark of the whole country. And this is justified. It symbolizes that partic-

ular Australian airiness, but also the successful incorporation of the Australian art of construction into the natural environment. This is what makes this country so special. Even though there were many fights during the development phase of the Opera House, which was designed by the Danish architect Jørn Utzon, and finally completed by an Australian Group of architects, it remains a fascinating construction, a picture which jumps to everybody's mind whenever one thinks about Australia. Its special fascination is based on Utzon's philosophy that buildings and their environment are

65

strongly interlinked. Here at Sydney Cove, at Bennelong Point, they seem to be particularly intense. Thus the Opera House manages to combine earth and water, the wind carries

noises and sounds out to sea and creates a magic environment around the building. Utzon stepped back from the project in exasperation in 1966, when there were serious complaints about the construction costs which had increased to 100 million dollars, but not without suggesting that they just go ahead and rip it all down again. A further seven years had to pass until it could be opened ceremoniously by Queen Elisabeth II. As a gesture of reconciliation, Utzon was given the contract to supervise the renovation works in 1999. Whether the construction of a high rise building of offices and apartments on East Circular Quay which was permitted in 1996, and which now towers over the Opera, destroys the total ensemble or

not is up to you to decide. It certainly does not contribute to the aesthetics. Even its nickname "Toaster" can provide little consolation.

Not only the large public buildings, skyscrapers and cultural monuments in the large cities of Perth, Melbourne, Sydney or Canberra, whose town planning is highly interesting, are impressive. The diversity and creativity of the architecture "down under" is also reflected in the smaller living spaces all around the country. Important elements of everyday architecture are the inspirations and the materials that are supplied by nature. Leading architects in the country integrate them into their plans. A unique Australian style implies discovering Asian, European and American influences and

using high-tech materials as well as increasingly wood and natural stones. Corrugated iron, which we do not use much anymore, is used a lot by one of the stars of the Australian architectural scene, Glenn Murcutt. In 1970, Murcutt reintroduced this very Australian construction material, which the settlers used back in the 19th century. It was his chosen material for the construction of houses of

impressively in the Architecture Design Studio of the University of Newcastle, 160 kilometers (100 miles) north of Sydney. The combination of steel and wood elements with the natural environment is fine and sensitive at the same time. Alex Popov also reflects upon the living conditions within and outside of cities. He prefers natural materials, such as sandstone, wood and copper and uses them to construct a

open, light designs. Since 1983 he has built several very unique houses, made completely of corrugated iron, which stand in perfect harmony with nature. The gentle wave-like lines, which are considered puristic today, together with the straight, functional type of construction, the play of light and shadow and the connection of the interior and exterior via broad verandas, render his buildings – whether a house in the bush, pavilion studios or the visitor's center of the Kakadu National Park – incomparably and timelessly elegant and functional. Other protagonists, such as James Grose from Brisbane, try to marry their preference for industrial design with the traditions of bush construction. Grose succeeded to do so

completely new concept of row house settlements, such as Mona Vale. The courtyards are designed as village squares – meeting places for the people living there. Whether it is a former penal village or a cosmopolitan metropolis, a bush camp or a colonial building, it is worth having a proper look at Australia's architecture.

Neo-baroque Princess Theatre and skyscrapers: sightseeing in Melbourne aboard the Circle Tram (left page, top). – Adventurous roof constructions in the Olympic Park in Sydney (large photograph). – The Seven Spirit Wilderness Lodge in Seven Spirit Bay (far left). – Sydney's Victorian suburb Paddington (left).– "Woolloomooloo W-Hotel" in Sydney (above).

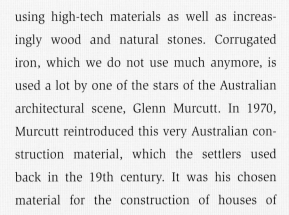

Sydney's Opera House combines water, land and architecture harmoniously (above). – Just married, at Brighton Beach (center). Eucalyptus trees and waterfalls in Barrington Tops National Park (below and right).

NEW SOUTH WALES VICTORIA

SYDNEY
BLUE MOUNTAINS
MELBOURNE
CANBERRA
GREAT OCEAN ROAD

The biggest attraction of Port Campbell National Park, a coastal strip
adjacent to the Great Ocean Road, is
the Twelve Apostles. At sunrise and
sunset the sun dips these rock formations in a lovely red light.

Surf lifesavers at Bondi Beach (left). – The sculptor William Rickets dedicated mystical monuments in the Dandenong Ranges to the Aborigines (center). – Seafood is very popular in Melbourne (right).

The southeast with the states New South Wales and Victoria provide a most delightful introduction to the diversity of Australia. Pulsating cities, lush rainforests, extensive beaches, mountain regions and red deserts form a kaleidoscope which you will fall in love with.

Let's face it – New South Wales does not exactly sound like a breathtaking natural environment with cosmopolitan cities and stunning landscapes. It sounds more like an attempt to transplant a piece of the rainy homeland into the Pacific. But that was hardly the intention of Captain James Cook when he discovered this large unknown island in 1770 by orders of the British Crown. Although apparently the coastline did remind him of Wales, solid economic interests were paramount, even at that time. The availability of new land for settlers, raw materials, prisoner colonies and whatever else was on the political agenda of the late 18th century, supported the development of New South Wales to become today's "Premier State". This title is used with a certain amount of pride: this is the oldest, economically strongest state of Australia with most inhabitants and the highest population density. It goes without saying that it is the most glamorous and trendiest state, too. But it is also one of the smallest states of Australia, with an area of just over 800,000 square kilometers (approx. 310,000 square miles). However, approximately a third of the total population of the fifth continent, around 6.4 million people, live here in the southeast. The name "Gateway to Australia" has a better ring to it and is also better suited. Sydney, the capital of New South Wales and host of the Olympic Games 2000, is regularly nominated as one of the cities in the world with the highest quality of life. The environs of the city are remarkable, too: the Blue Mountains, the gorgeous beaches for

the surfers, the vineyards of the Hunter Valley or the numerous national parks.

Whoever sets foot on Australian ground for the first time, after touching down in Sydney following a grueling 25 hour flight, will want to take it easy and get used to the time difference of nine plus hours. But there is no time for that in Sydney. You will immediately be mesmerized by the flair of this cosmopolitan city. Australia's oldest and largest city of almost four million leaves you no time to sleep. A good way of driving away the fatigue is to take a trip around the harbor and to start to get your bearings in a city that is impressive and cosmopolitan at the same time. Sunny, sexy, chic – there is something about Sydney's image. You will need at least three days to start to get a feel for this city with its very special flair. The famous Opera House and Harbour Bridge, the Rocks, a part of town where the European settlement started, the busy city center with its shopping meccas, such as the "Strand Arcade", and the boutiques in Double Bay and Paddington. And of course you need to visit "Bondi Beach", the best known of the thirty beaches in the city area. Relax on the beach before diving into one of the night clubs in Kings Cross or strolling through the City Night Market in Dixon Street, Haymarket. Fortunately the countryside is not very far, as after so much nightlife you will feel like recuperating in the great outdoors.

Sydney is practically enclosed by national parks. Royal National Park, Australia's oldest park, lies only 15 kilometers (approx. 9 miles) south of the city. But the proximity of this park can also be quite disconcerting. In the devastating bush fires in 2002, a total of 650,000 hectares of forest and farmland were lost

The Three Sisters stand proud at Echo Point in the Blue Mountain National Park (left page). Koalas feed on the leaves of certain types of eucalyptus.

and the flames came threateningly close to the city. Only about a 40 minute drive north lies the Ku-Ring-Gai Chase National Park along the banks of the Hawkesbury River. From the lookout point West Head you get a good view of the grandiose forests and bush and the rugged coastline. In the center of the national park, in the Waratah Wildlife Park, you can stroke koalas and kangaroos. You can admire Aboriginal rock engravings on the Basin and Echidna

In Old Sydney Town on the Pacific Highway near Gosford, the history of Sydney is reenacted in the museum village (below). Victoria also looks after its historical heritage, here in Sovereign Hill (left).

Tracks. The Blue Mountains, which are only 90 minutes away from the city, are very attractive too, and not only for Sydneysiders. Here you will find everything that the outdoor heart desires: eucalyptus forests and bizarre rock formations as far as the eye can see, waterfalls, stalactite caves and steep gorges, rainforests and romantic valleys with fruit plantations and farmland. Picturesque places, such as Leura and Katoomba, Wentworth Falls or Glenbrook, wait to be discovered. And the Three Sisters, of course, which should not be confused with the Twelve Apostles

in the neighboring state Victoria. These sisters – Gunedoo, Wimlah and Meenhi – were a little naughty. According to the legend, they were turned into the three cliffs by a wizard when they started to get involved with three men. At Echo Point you can get very close to the Three Sisters with the cable car. You will see for yourself how attractive they are to this day, as countless mountaineers still try to conquer them. This wilderness of 247,000 hectares was declared the Greater Blue Mountain World Heritage Area by UNESCO in 2000, together with the adjacent national parks Kanangra-Boyd in the southwest and Wollemi in the north. The entire World Heritage Area has a size of more than one million hectares. In it you can go bush walking, climbing, canyoning to your heart's delight or take a course in survival training, far from any civilization. The wild canyons of the Jamison Valley, with the 961 steps of the Giant Stairway leading down to them (unfortunately they also have to be climbed up again), and the

ways, which meander from Cape Howe in the south up to Tweed Heads in the north. These coastal roads were given the number "one" for a reason. They are not only first class in terms of the views they offer, but also in terms of the wind, water and wave conditions for surfers. The Pacific Coast Highway extends from Sydney to Brisbane, a length of 979 kilometers (approx. 610 miles). So far, everybody has found his or her perfect wave or his

Jenolan Caves, an extensive cave labyrinth, come close to true natural wonders. And New South Wales even caters for those who enjoy winter sports. Between July and September, when there is enough snow, almost everyone who is able to keep on his or her skis flocks to the Snowy Mountains in the south of the state and particularly to Mount Kosciusko, the highest mountain in Australia, 2,228 meters (7,308 feet) high.

You will see those boards which are a little broader, but no less sporty, everywhere along the Princes and the Pacific Coast High-

The gold digger period of the 19th century is kept alive in Ballarat (above).
The open-air museum "Sovereign Hill" makes the Victorian period come alive. Everything is authentic – from the costumes to the bakery (left).

or her perfect beach at Byron Bay, where sub-tropical rainforest meets white sand and turquoise water. But the south coast, too, has no less to offer. You fill find some of the best beaches along Stanley Park. Particularly in the Jervis Bay region there are beaches such as Hyams Beach which has the reputation of having the whitest sand on Earth. And this takes us to the special case Canberra, as Jervis Bay is governed from here. When in 1901

The Puffin Billy Railway chugs along from Belgrave to Gembrook (above). – Beautiful blossoms (above). The Great Ocean Road cuts through the northern part of the Ottway National Park (right).

the Australian colonies joined together to form the Commonwealth of Australia, one could not decide whether Melbourne or Sydney should be the capital city. With true Australian pragmatism, an area of 2,368 square kilometers (approx. 914 square miles) in the Limestone Plains, south of Yass, was carved out of New South Wales and was henceforth called "Australian Capital Territory" (ACT). Canberra, which means "meeting point" in the Aboriginal language, was created, too. It became the future seat for government and the new capital of the country. To this day, Canberra cannot quite get rid of its slightly artificial character, but some of the prejudices are no longer justified. Not only the National Gallery of Australia and Old Parliament House, which is possibly the most beautiful, neoclassical building in the entire country, are worth seeing. A proper leisure area has developed right in the center of town, all around Lake Burley Griffin, an artificial lake around 11 kilometers (7 miles) long. However, seen from here Capitol Hill really does look a little ostentatious.

It is finer elsewhere, around 130 kilometers (80 miles) north of Sydney. In the Hunter Valley around eighty wineries have contributed to its reputation of being the best winegrowing region in New South Wales. And despite this also being one of the largest coal mining regions in Australia. But that obviously did not frighten the winegrowers off. Here they produce excellent Chardonnays, Sémillons and the red Shiraz which can be tasted in small wine-tasting rooms in picturesque villages such as Cessnock and Singleton and which bring the atmosphere of rural Australia during the colonial period back to life. Upper and Lower Hunter Valley have become a popular destination, particularly each October when the festival "Jazz in the Vines" is held. Some of the Sémillons are as dry as the country at the other end of New South Wales. In the west lies Broken Hill, at the border to New South Wales. The Indian Pacific railway stops here and this is also the headquarters of the world famous Flying Doctors. The Royal Flying Doctor Service, which was founded in 1928 by Reverend John Flynn, has saved many people's lives. And from here, in the middle of the outback, the "School of the Air" is run, too. It supplies children on remote farms in a region of 800,000 square kilometers (310,000 square miles) with education and schooling. This soothes the fact that this place "in the middle of nowhere" has shrunk to two thirds of its former size. Here, 1,200 kilometers (745 miles) west of Sydney, 30,000 people lived off silver and ore mines in the 1960s. Today an energetic artist colony which has settled here has, at least for the time being, protected Broken

The high plateau in Mount Buffalo National Park with its bizarre rock formations protrudes from the valleys and forests like a moon landscape (left). – Here you can go on long hikes through dense forests and bush in bloom (above).

Hill from the same fate of a ghost town as can be seen in neighboring Silverton. Aside from that, the film industry has chosen this desolate region as one of their favorite locations. Blockbusters such as "Mad Max 2", "A Town Like Alice" and "Priscilla – Queen of the Desert" were filmed here. The only thing that is missing is a theme park called "Life on the Moon". But then this idea may be implemented sooner than you can imagine.

Bizarre basalt formations are found in the Alpine National Park. In winter it is a popular area for skiers (left). – Wilsons Promontory used to be a land bridge, connecting Australia with Tasmania (below).

In Victoria, too, visitors are spoilt by the most varied landscapes, natural events and great hospitality. Victoria is the second smallest state, but it is still as large as the UK. Just under five million people, of which 3.5 million alone live in the wider area of Melbourne, enjoy the temperate climate here which still offers them four proper seasons. Throughout the majority of Australia you merely have the "wet" or the "dry season".

Coming from New South Wales via the Princes Highway you will arrive at Lakes Entrance first. This is a very popular holiday resort for families with kids. Its name is derived from the fact that here the extensive network of rivers and lakes of the "Gippsland",

with its national parks Baw Baw and Tarra-Bulga, has created the one and only access to the sea. The dune landscape of Ninety Mile Beach and it's endless, albeit quite dangerous beaches have become the holiday destination par excellence. Croajingolong National Park is located more tranquilly, hidden away at the eastern tip of Victoria. It is still almost a well-kept secret. Due to its uniqueness, UNESCO has declared it a Biosphere Reserve. It contains pristine forests, heathland, high sand dunes, sea inlets which extend far into the interior, and lonely bays. And in the middle there is the picturesque fishing village Mallacoota, a place where time seems to have stood still. "Wilsons Promontory

National Park, which is usually referred to as "Wilsons Prom", at the southern tip of Victoria is much better known and is consequently frequented more as well. Here, too, you experience the contrasts of nature in a relatively small area: white beaches and steep cliffs, dense rainforest and extensive hilly landscapes. This is the habitat of more than 190 bird species. Tidal River is the headquarters of the park rangers. In its visitors' center you can

the most European of all Australian cities. It combines British-Victorian charm with a southern lifestyle. With its fashion, culture and food festivals, its sports events and its impressive number of city parks and gardens, it is Sydney's eternal rival. As the city lies on both sides of the mouth of the Yarra, a boat trip on the Yarra River is worthwhile. But to get a good view, you can also climb high up onto the viewing platform of the Rialto Tower on the 55th

obtain information on its flora and fauna. Half way to Melbourne lies Phillip Island, which is proud to have Victoria's most famous tourist attraction: the Penguin Parade. Every year 3.5 million visitors (the same amount of people who live in Melbourne) flock here to admire the cute parade which is performed every evening when the penguins return from their hunt for food and march back to their nests on the beach.

Melbourne, the second largest city in Australia and which hosted the Olympic Games in 1956, has grown to become a city of 3.5 million and it still attracts Greeks, Italians, Americans or Asians, as it represents a multicultural melting pot. Melbourne is

Hidden bays in Wilsons Promontory National Park, such as Refuge Cove, can only be accessed on foot (above). If you take a hike between Refuge Cove and Waterloo Bay you will experience stunning sections of the coastline, such as here in "Wilsons Prom" (left).

St. Kilda, a coastal suburb, attracts Melburnians and tourists alike for a Sunday walk or to relax in one of its countless cafés along the promenade.

story. You won't believe your eyes: there really is a sports stadium or a park in every corner of the city. There are over sixty golf courses, football stadiums, tennis courts for the Australian Open, the course for the Formula One race: a city for sports enthusiasts. You can do without a hire car by catching a free ride around the city center with the red City Circle Tram, whilst being allowed to get on and off wherever and how often you like. If you get off at Flinders Station and walk along the path which takes you over Princes Bridge, you will get to the Royal Botanic Gardens, which are certainly amongst the most beautiful parks in the world. Ferdinand von Müller, a German botanist, played a key role in setting out the gardens which have a size of 40 hectares. Today it contains more than 1,000 rare plants, ancient avenues of trees, flower gardens, picturesque lakes and river courses, cafés and rest areas. White Como House with its garden from the colonial times is also an oasis of tranquility in the middle of this large city. You will find the last Australian manor house of the 19th century, which is still owned privately, in Rippon Lee in the part of town called Elsternwick. It is not only its architecture which is charming. You will be awed by its orchards, its ponds, its combination of English and Asian garden traditions, its evenings of chamber music and garden parties. Then it's off for a shopping spree in the Victorian Block Arcade, on Swanston Walk and the many laneways, the small 19th century alleys, where the trendy boutiques are to be found. A stroll over Queen Victoria Market will be a culinary trip of discovery. Finally, a good place to gently end a day in Melbourne is the Bellavista Social Club in Crossley Street.

Melbourne had its first heyday in the middle of the 19th century, in the time of the gold rush. However, the real center of the gold rush was Ballarat, around 110 kilometers (68 miles) further west. Ballarat is the most famous gold diggers' town in Australia. On the way there you get an impression of the seemingly endless expanse of the country. There are only few settlements in this red sandy steppe in between dense forests. Above all of it is a vast sky with fantastic cloud formations. Ballarat, a city of 70,000, has a Wildlife Park where you can stroke koalas and kangaroos, and Sovereign Hill, the reconstructed gold diggers' town. Here you can try to wash gold yourself, visit original mines and watch the multimedia show "Blood on the Southern Cross" which includes goose bumps and crocodile tears. It is a reminder of the Eureka Stockade of 1854, when the poor fortune hunters rose up against far too costly digging rights and corrupt government officials. This

See page 88

Lady with hat, gentleman with hat, spectator with hat: whatever the weather, whether it rains or snows, whether there is a storm blowing or the sun is shining, you do not go to the Melbourne Cup Carnival without a hat. Well, yes, the sunglasses, the suit, the tie and the shoes also make a difference. But the hat is the all important fashion attribute for any nomination of the most beautiful and graceful throughout this Cup fever. So they have to be works of art. And no, horses will not have to race wearing hats soon, that is just a rumor. Beautiful, yes indeed …

MELBOURNE
AND ITS COMPLETELY CRAZY HORSE RACE

Two things which make Melbourne one of the most interesting cities in Australia are its creative design scene and its large sports events. What's so particularly trendy about this multicultural city with its over 3.4 million inhabitants on the Yarra River? The largest Greek community outside of Athens, the many designer shops? King prawns and pasta in Vertigo, Brunswick Street, Fitzroy or a glass of Shiraz from the Warrenmang vineyards in Walter's Wine Bar in Southgate during the "Food and Wine Festival"? Melbourne does not rely on previous glories, but celebrates its present strengths.

And there are so many of them that the annual Australian Grand Prix in Albert Park, with its Formula One circus and the racing car heroes, is not even the main event. Nor is it the Football Final or the Australian Open tennis championships. No, the Australians do not hold their breath until that special early afternoon

on the first Tuesday in November. That is when real horsepower is called for at Flemington Racecourse. Whoever states that all Melburnians love sports is understating it: all Melburnians are crazy about sports! And on the day of the grand Cup, which is a bank holiday by the way, everyone goes absolutely mad! The magic formula is: Melbourne Cup! People start preparing for it a month ahead to select the most fantastic outfit for the big day. The Cup is a parade of hats, suits, dresses and ties. You will see all styles here – modern, traditional and avant-garde.

The horse race fever started in 1861. Originally the race was held over a distance of 2 miles. Since 1972, the horses have had to cover the longer distance of 3,200 meters (2 miles) before they have a chance to obtain fame and honor. Famous winning horses were Archer, who won the race in 1861, Carbine (1890) and Phar Lap (1930). To this day every Australian knows

Melbourne's Princes Bridge (above left). – The horses are the true stars of the Melbourne Cup (left). High bets are placed on them on racing day (right). Cricket cannot keep up with this big event (above). It is as crowded in Elizabeth Street as it is on the racetracks (large photograph).

them, not only because they were particularly handsome horses and outsiders, but also because they won the race so impressively.

This is a style which the Australians love in sports. Of course there are lots of parties after the races – in the city and in the parks. The Melbourne Cup Carnival fits so well to this city, because it is all about green grass – on the racecourse and during the parties afterwards. There won't be another city of millions in the world with as many parks. They are all used as catwalks. Picnics are held under their tea trees and on the banks of their ponds. Alexis, an Australian of Greek descent, explains the secret of this city: "In Melbourne you can truly live. People still have time, they are peaceful and friendly. This is all thanks to the Melbourne Cup Carnival where they all let their hair down."

Melbourne's skyline on the Yarra
River is softened by bridges, green
spaces and parks. The river, which
was long neglected, has now been
cleaned up and made more attractive (left). – Flinders Street Station,
which was built at the beginning
of the 20th century, is a popular
starting point for city tours, as this
is where the suburban trains leave
in all directions (above).

protest, which was defeated by force, is considered the only armed rebellion in the history of Australia. For many Australians it signifies the beginning of the democratic development of the country, as the rebels were discharged and the gold licenses were abolished.

You will get a real feel for Victoria's natural treasures if you drive another 150 kilometers (93 miles) west into the Grampians

Albury, on the border between New South Wales and Victoria, with its charming pubs, is a popular place to take a break (left). – There are remains of a dried out lake in Mungo National Park (below).

National Park. This densely forested mountain region, which was formed 400 million years ago by earthquakes, is a hikers' paradise of mythical rock formations, caves and Aboriginal cult sites. With the help of a pair of binoculars, you can spot koalas, kangaroos, echidnas, possums, parrots and cockatoos. In Halls Gap, practically the gateway to the Grampians, equipped with all necessary amenities for tourists, you will come across people like David Sears, the former professional player of the Melbourne Hawthornes, who has swapped the roaring of 50,000 fans in the stadiums of the Australian Football League with the tranquility and remoteness of the Grampians National Park. In his cabin

resort on the foot of the mountains he tells us about his new life enthusiastically: "We have wonderful hiking trails here with fantastic views and it is so unbelievably quiet at night." He grills kangaroo steak and emu sausages on the barbecue and later, when we all sit around the camp fire together, he tells his stories of rough matches and tough men: "Many teeth were lost and you only got new ones at the end of your career. It wouldn't have been worth it anyway earlier – the matches were real tough!" It is also worth organizing a day trip to the small, but fine wine region of the Pyrenees. Although a Shiraz or a Riesling from the Barossa Valley is considered Australia's best wine, it is worth visiting the smaller vineyards, such as Warrenmang in Moonambel or the Montara Vinery in Ararat. If you try a Bazzani Chardonnay or a Montare Pinot Noir here, you will be surprised: these are wines of great character, true southern stars.

What Sisters are for some, Apostles are for others. And the famous twelve are even located along one of the most beautiful coastal roads worldwide. The road was built in the 1920s to pro-

played an important role in the development of the hinterland. Even today it supplies water for agricultural uses along its banks, but it has also been expanded as a leisure region. Muscat grapes, which make superb wines, grow in Mildura on the Murray River. It is too good to use it as sacramental wine, may the Apostles forgive me. But they make you come very close to paradise on Earth in New South Wales and Victoria.

vide access to Adelaide. It meanders along the 250-kilometer (155-mile) stretch of Victoria's southern coast from Geelong via the surfers' paradise Torquay, the beach resort Lorne and the fishing village Apollo Bay to Warrnambool where you can watch whales between May and October. Maybe these twelve bizarre rock formations close to the coast also remind us to respect nature more. Next to Sydney's Opera House and Uluru, they are surely the most popular photo motif.

The Murray River forms almost the entire northern Victorian border to New South Wales. With 2,575 kilometers (1,600 miles) length, it is the longest river in Australia. In the 19th century it

On the way to Cooma, the main town of the Snowy Mountains, travelers will come across these smoothly-weathered sandstone cliffs (above). In Broken Hill there are still many miners who will show you around the mine.

Warrumbungle National Park is
famous for its huge "Gras Trees"
(above) and for its rich flora and
fauna. The mountains, including
Bluff Mountain west of Coonabaran-
bran, are of volcanic origin and are
more than thirteen million years old
(right). – Following double page:
Sydney with its many bays as seen
from above. Opera House, Harbour
Bridge and the City. The Tasman
Sea in the background.

CITY OF DREAMS

"EASY GOING" IN SYDNEY

The winner is: Sydney!" When the decision was made which country was allowed to host the Olympic Games in 2000, a whole nation went mad. Australia and especially Sydney celebrated this historic event on the streets day and night for several days. It

moved the continent and the metropolis on Port Jackson into the focus of global attention again. Not only sports enthusiasts made their way to Sydney, but so did nature lovers who used the Olympic Games as an additional incentive to discover a country with its secret capital city which has become synonymous with freedom, adventure and "easy living".

What is the best way to explore such a city? There are two possibilities: either you let yourself drift and have faith in coincidences, or you go down the beaten tracks which will always lead you to the main attractions. Like so many

things in life, the middle way is the best. This means you should get off the streets and onto a boat, as the best way to see Sydney is from the sea. A harbor tour with "Matilda Cruises" will show you the panorama of this city which is as cosmopolitan as it is multicultural. Some

140 different ethnic groups live in this city of four million. It has about half a million more inhabitants than Berlin, but it is about twelve times the size. A harbor tour leaving from Darling Harbor or Sydney Cove will take you to beaches kilometers long, to bays and marinas as well as to Harbour Bridge and the famous Opera House. A skyline will unravel itself before your eyes, symbolizing the character of this city: generous and positive, elegant and playful. Even in the busy city center it is relaxed. People take time to have a chat. "How are you today" is not just an empty phrase here.

In 1788, the "First Fleet" dropped anchor at Circular Quay. Today the ferries depart from here and romantic rendezvous are held in the street cafés (left). Harbour Bridge dominates The Rocks, the meeting point for nightlife. Nowadays drunken guys are no longer kidnapped and brought onto the ships (large photo). – Between business towers and Sydney Tower: you get a wonderful view of Darling Harbour from the monorail (right page, top). – You reach North Sydney via Harbour Bridge. Here you find areas which have kept the charm of glamorous resorts of the past.

A friendly manner of dealing with one another is part of the cultivated lifestyle. It makes no difference if it is a friend or a stranger. This is a sign of a special culture. And Sydney really is a remarkable city of museums which has managed not to elevate culture and reverentially hide it behind walls, but to integrate it into the life of the various parts of the city. The Australian Museum on Hyde Park in College Street is home to the largest collection of natural history of the continent: here you can see minerals and fossils, stuffed birds and mammals which are now extinct, but also an interesting exhibition on the Australian Aborigines and the indigenous people of Papua New Guinea. Outside, in front of the museum, Hyde Park is busy, but relaxed, at lunchtime. The Sydneysiders love to have their lunch outdoors and this park, which is centrally located right next to the Central Business District, is just the right place to have a lunch break, particularly as its tall trees provide cool shade. This is a lovely spot to relax, especially as the weather is usually gorgeous. Sydney has 342 sunny days a year. If you want to experience a culinary high, climb Sydney Tower, which is 325 meters (1,066 feet) high, have a snack or a cup of coffee in the revolving restaurant at a height of 305 meters (1,000 feet) and enjoy the view over the harbor, the city and the Blue Mountains. From the Tower it is only a hop, skip and a jump to the Domain, which consists of the Botanic Gardens and Hyde Park and is the largest green lung of the city. Here, art and nature harmonize, too. The Art Gallery of New South Wales, a mighty sandstone building at the east end of the park, contains masterpieces of Australian art of the 19th and 20th century. You should also spend some time in the Asian and Aboriginal collections. After so much art and culture it is nice to go for a walk through the Royal Botanic Gardens which have a lovely setting around Farm Cove. From the lookout point known as Mrs. Macquarie's Chair you can see Fort Denison, a small penal island which was established in 1855 and which you can now access by boats from Circular Quay. As the story goes, this lookout point used to be a place for the governor's wife to withdraw to. From here she supposedly longingly watched the ships leaving the harbor. The Botanic Gar-

tances of many kilometers. Part of the gardens is used as an open-air cinema in the summer and concerts are regularly held in the magnificent building of the Conservatory for Music. On your list of museums you must not forget the National Maritime Museum in Darling Harbour, which takes you through the past and the present of this seafaring nation, and the Powerhouse Museum, which offers an attractive mixture of technology, social history and history of art. It is particularly popular with families with kids. The Museum of Contemporary Art at Circular Quay, The Rocks, rounds off the cultural trip of Sydney nicely. Here a collection of works of international artists of the 20th century and a large area of traditional Aboriginal art presents modernity which has actually almost become history now.

dens do not only have exotic and rare plants, they are also the resting place for a sizeable colony of flying foxes, those bats which hang in the crowns of trees sleeping during the day and hunt for food at night, while covering dis-

The Rocks are the oldest part of Sydney. This historic dockland area, where the first white settlers set foot on firm ground in 1788, had a bad reputation from the start. Thirty years ago, the government finally wanted to demolish the

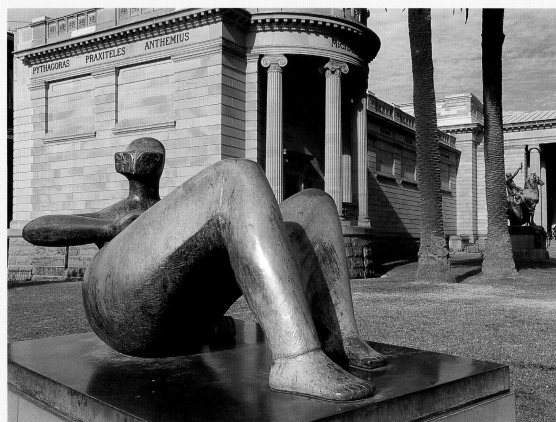

remaining buildings. But heavy protests achieved a little miracle: instead of demolishing the place, the city restored the area and now the former eyesore has become a smart part of town complete with restaurants, pubs, bars and boutiques. A walk over the cobblestones through the narrow alleys, past colonial architecture and numerous galleries and pubs will rekindle the atmosphere of past centuries. Whoever wants to be "in" in Sydney, will live in dreadfully expensive Paddington where a house will easily cost a million dollars. Another cool address is Oxford Street, the colorful gay area of town. Neighboring Surrey Hills is also popular amongst young artists, creative people and cosmopolites. Here, many of the Victorian town houses have been restored and all around Crown Street smart restaurants, cool bars and alternative markets have opened up. The formerly run-down dockland areas Woolloomooloo and Kings Cross have also become presentable today thanks to an interesting pub and theater scene. And you can spend months

exploring the best shopping areas, the most beautiful surf beaches and the most sumptuous food temples. But you simply have to pop into the Queen Victoria Building, the three story cupola palace in the heart of the city on George Street and into the Strand Arcade, where all the famous designers of this world and the fashion talents of tomorrow have opened up shop. And you should not say farewell to the city on Port Jackson without having tested its waters. If you find the shark warnings along the beaches disconcerting, you can calmly bathe in one of the rock pools which have been cut into the cliffs or in the Andrew Charlton Pool next to Mrs. Macquarie's Chair, the lookout of a former governor's wife.

At the market in The Rocks you will find everything from arts and crafts, souvenirs to opals (left page).
In the Queen Victoria Building you can spend a lot of money in some 200 exclusive shops (large photograph).
You will find this sculpture of Henry Moore in front of the Art Gallery of New South Wales (above).

Wineglass Bay, Freycinet National Park, is a beach walker's heaven (above), South West National Park (center) is the same for hikers. – Franklin Wharf in Hobart is a picture-book harbor (below). Richmond has a lot of flair (right).

TASMANIA

HOBART
CRADLE MOUNTAIN LAKE ST. CLAIR
NATIONAL PARK
PORT ARTHUR

The Huon Valley near Franklin
is an ideal territory for nature
lovers and sailors. This photograph shows it in a type of light
which is typical for Tasmania.

Tasmanian impressions: fishermen loading their lobster pots (left), prison church in Port Arthur (center) and a Banksia in Freycinet National Park (right).

Tasmania fascinates its visitors with its green, pristine natural environment. The small Victorian towns and of course the warm-hearted "Tassies", the hospitable inhabitants themselves, contribute to the very special charm of Tasmania.

It was always hard for little Tasmania to step out of the mighty shadow of the mother continent, Australia, even though it is only an hour's flight away. But now more and more visitors are also attracted to the southern-most tip of "down under". But that is not surprising: the whole of Tasmania has fewer inhabitants than Austin, Texas in an area as large as that of the entire Republic of Ireland, resulting in the very low population density of six inhabitants per square kilometer. Fortunately, millions of sheep and cattle serve as live motifs for hobby filmmakers in this beautiful landscape, devoid of people. Aside from milk and wool, the main Tasmanian products are potatoes, apples and onions plus seafood, including abalone (a quarter of the world's total harvest), salmon, oysters, mussels, brown trout and lobster. Almost 30 percent of the country enjoys national park status, 20 percent of it has been placed on UNESCO's prestigious World Heritage List. Thanks to its maritime humid climate and active environmental associations, an almost pristine wilderness can grow wild. Around 10 percent of the total area of Tasmania is covered by dense rainforests. Particularly in the southwest there are still large areas that have not been explored and developed yet. This is why this part of Tasmania is sometimes called by its mystical name "Never-Never-Land." In Tasmania's treasure trove of enchanting natural features you will find rainforests in magic mountain ranges as well as gorgeous coasts and beaches and idyllic fishing harbors in picturesque bays. The "Tassies" claim that Tasmania's air is cleaner than anywhere else in the world. Narrow

Heathland in the Cradle Mountain Lake St. Clair National Park near "Waldheim" (left page). A Tasmanian Devil in Trowunna Wildlife Park (above).

"Bass Strait", which separates Tasmania from the continent, is held partially responsible for this. This is where the "Roaring Forties", the howling winds of the 40th latitude, blow in full force. The winds are so strong in this passage, which is 250 kilometers (155 miles) wide, that over seventy ships have capsized here so far, leading to the loss of around one thousand human lives by drowning. Therefore, sailing regattas between Sydney and Hobart count as one of the toughest tests. When Charles Darwin had just survived this treacherous stretch of water on his sailing trip around the world and was on his approach to Tasmania's coast, he made the following entry in his logbook, a description of the rough arrival in Tasmanian waters: "On the 5th of February, after a six days' passage, of which the first part was fine, and the latter very cold and squally, we entered the mouth of Storm Bay: the weather justified this awful name." You cannot compare the Tasmanian climate with the warmer climate of mainland Australia. As the seasons are the other way around here in the southern hemisphere, a rough Tasmanian autumn often starts around Easter. It may be magnificently disguised as an "Indian Summer", but often brings cold and wet weather. Even Tasmanian summers are unpredictable, it can rain a lot. This is why Tasmania is so lush and green. In any case you can experience the climate of Italy, Scotland, California and Oregon here, all at once in the course of a single morning. Tasmania has all climatic zones, all forms of vegetation and all landscape types. At least that is what the "Tassies" claim. "Tassies" – this is how the Tasmanian inhabitants who have immigrated from all over the world like to call themselves. Almost every second "Tassie" lives in Hobart, the capital. If he ever had to emigrate, then he would emigrate to this place. Apparently these were the words of young Darwin when he set sight on Hobart when he sailed into its port in 1836 aboard the "Beagle". In his travel log "Voyage of the Beagle" he documented his first impressions: "Late in the evening we anchored in the snug cove, on the shores of which stands the capital of Tasmania. The first aspect of the place was very inferior to that of Sydney; the latter might be called a

Hobart's Battery Point used to be the stomping ground for seamen and fishermen during the colonial times. Today you can admire its finely restored Georgian architecture (left). Lobster pots on the jetty of Hobart's Franklin Wharf (below).

city, this is only a town. It stands at the base of Mount Wellington, a mountain 3100 feet high, but of little picturesque beauty; from this source, however, it receives a good supply of water. Round the cove there are some fine warehouses and on one side a small fort." Australia's oldest barracks, the "Anglesea Barracks" which were built in 1811, were already an important military base when Darwin arrived here. And at that time you could already admire ferns, roses and a little later, in 1818, even a Japanese garden in Hobart's Botanical Gardens. From 1831 onwards, the nobler social circles held their functions in Secheron House, which is now home to the Tasmanian Maritime Museum, while

Narryna House was still being completed. Narryna House is now "Van Diemen's Land Folk Museum", which documents the life of the early settlers with old furniture, paintings and porcelain. During Darwin's visit to Hobart, hundreds of prisoners were still laboring on the construction of the Theatre Royal. And when the curtain of Australia's oldest stage was finally lifted for the first time in 1837, Darwin had unfortunately already sailed off again. Just a few years later Hobart's Parliament House opened as the main customs office. It is one of the mightiest colonial buildings of the island capital. Not much has changed in the historic dockland area Battery Point, which had more or less been completed in 1804, since Darwin's visit. With its splendid architecture and beautifully restored facades of stately manor houses, which used to belong to the rich merchant families of the time, it is still one of the best residential addresses in Hobart. And where the stevedores, sailors and fishermen used to roam around, you can now enjoy a lovely harbor atmosphere. A city tour around this island metropolis with just under 200,000 inhabitants will lead you past

on Tasmanian land, they hunted the Aborigines like animals and wiped them out systematically. There were regular conflicts, as the new settlers built fences around grazing land for their cattle, thus claiming more and more land for themselves. Darwin's comments on this gruesome eradication campaign against the Aborigines were as follows: "I fear there is no doubt, that this train of evil and its consequences, originated in the infamous conduct of

the Central Post Office to the Town Hall, a sandstone building from 1864, and to Constitution Dock. Artists and galleries, bistros and trendy bars have moved into the historic warehouses at Salamanca Place and ensure a feel of urban worldliness on this last tip of the Earth. Visitors and locals alike enjoy the lively atmosphere of the Salamanca Markets where illustrious secondhand goods, books and antiques are on offer. Another one of Hobart's attractions is the "Tasmanian Museum and Art Gallery". Here, the main topic is Tasmania's history, in particular the colonial epoch and the fate of the indigenous population. The latter is a very sad chapter in the history of this island. When the Europeans set foot

Hobart is home to a flourishing art scene. On Franklin Wharf you can occasionally watch a painter at work (above). – Hobart's Town Hall is a mighty sandstone building. It was completed in 1864 and is situated directly opposite the equally splendid Central Post Office (left).

some of our countrymen." After all, after 1830, white men could kill Aborigines without being punished, when "the whole island … was put under martial law, and by proclamation the whole population commanded to assist in one great attempt to secure the entire race. The plan adopted was similar to that of the great hunting-matches in India: a line was formed reaching across the island, with the intention of driving the natives into a cul-de-

Duck pond in Bushy Park (top). The owner of the "Blacksmith Gallery" in Sheffield likes to take it easy (above). View of Launceston, Tasmania's "Garden City" (right page). View of Hobart (following double page).

sac on Tasman's peninsula." The Aborigines which were caught during such hunts were transported to Flinders Island in the Bass Strait where they vegetated away on mission stations and frequently contracted European diseases and died. The body of a dead Aboriginal woman was preserved just like that of an animal and was displayed to the public.

Leaving Hobart you can take the Arthur Highway towards the Tasman Peninsula. You drive through dense forests and the first place along the way is Richmond, a jewel of colonial architecture. This small town between Hobart and Port Arthur was an important strategic post up until 1872 and is considered the best preserved colonial place on the island. Hobart is proud of the fact that it is home to Australia's finest collection of early Georgian buildings, but Richmond can be just as proud. Its Main Street is adorned with lovely houses of the 19th century and it has two superlatives: Richmond Bridge, constructed in 1825, is Australia's oldest bridge and St. John's Roman Catholic Church, built in 1837, is Australia's oldest Catholic church. It is fortunate that the arrival of modern Australia took such a long time, due to the remoteness of this island. Therefore many of the lovely old buildings were spared demolition. This is also why there is no other Australian holiday region with more historic bed & breakfasts and inns than in Tasmania.

At Eaglehawk Neck, the Tasman Peninsula rises out of the sea with massive granite cliffs. This is the place where, hidden in idyllic bays, the boats of some of the town people are tied up in front of rustic weekend cabins. Then, on the approach to Port Arthur, the traffic often gets heavier. Busses, hire cars and campers are on their way to Tasmania's number one attraction, to the penitentiary. Thousands of prisoners convicted to hard labor were brought here from England between 1830 and 1877. It was not hard to get a "ticket" to Port Arthur. The industrial revolution and the population explosion dramatically increased the crime rate in British towns and its prisons were bursting at the seams. The development of a new colony came just at the right time. Whoever committed the slightest crime was shipped overseas, such as 17-year old Samuel Sheepwash from Gloucester who was sentenced to fifteen years in 1852 only because he had stolen a pair of shoes. A 28 year-old plasterer from Wales, by the name of John Kerswell, faced the same fate, because he had stolen ten pounds and fifteen shillings.

Very few of the deported returned back home after they had served their sentence, that is if they survived their imprisonment

See page 115

ON THE TRAILS OF THE RANGERS

TREKKING IN THE TASMANIAN WILDERNESS

Visitors to Tasmania will experience wild rivers and deep canyons, rugged mountain ranges as well as rainforests with gigantic trees more than 1,000 years old. With its 1,600 meters (5,248 feet), Mount Ossa has the highest peak in the central mountain landscapes of the Cradle Mountain Lake St. Clair National Park.

not too long, the hikes take a couple of hours at the most and lead you through alpine landscapes or along extensive bays and beaches. The tracks of the Freycinet Peninsula Circuit lead you through the Freycinet National Park and provide views of the fantastic Hazards – red granite rocks which jut 300 meters (984 feet)

Tasmania has long been considered one of the top trekking destinations. There are a total of 3,000 kilometers (around 1865 miles) of tracks and 880 routes through the wilderness. The Tasmanian Parks & Wildlife Service has compiled a guide to the most beautiful trekking routes, sorted by region and degree of difficulty, complete with a description of the route, maps, approximate trekking times, places to stay for the night, advice regarding weather conditions and other useful pieces of information. Some of the trails are quite easy, such as Tasmania's Great Short Walks. The suggested routes are

out of the sea – and to famous Wineglass Bay, which has the reputation of being one of the most beautiful bays in the world. The Tasman Coastal Trail runs along the wild and rugged coast of the Tasman Peninsula with its strange rock formations near Eaglehawk Neck, such as Blowhole, Tasman Arch and Devil's Kitchen. For those hikers who are more experienced and are looking for a challenge, the Overland Hike is a nice 80-kilometer (50-mile) hike. It is split up into manageable daily sections and leads you through the Cradle Lake St. Clair National Park. It is the most famous hiking trail in Aus-

The Overland Track is the best known hiking trail in Tasmania. It leads through the Cradle Mountain Lake St. Clair National Park with a length of 80 kilometers (50 miles) (far right). – Reward for the effort: you get a fantastic view of Cradle Mountain and Dove Lake from Marion's Lookout (above). – A path through dense green: tree ferns seam the trail in the rainforest of Mount Field National Park (right). Along the Overland Track: signs show you the way; the hut is not only interesting for hikers, but for wallabies, too (right page). View of Strahan on the wide bay of Macquarie Harbour (following double page).

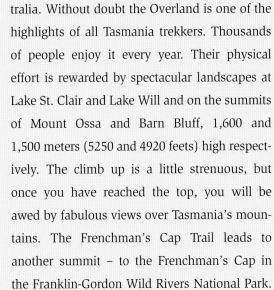

tralia. Without doubt the Overland is one of the highlights of all Tasmania trekkers. Thousands of people enjoy it every year. Their physical effort is rewarded by spectacular landscapes at Lake St. Clair and Lake Will and on the summits of Mount Ossa and Barn Bluff, 1,600 and 1,500 meters (5250 and 4920 feets) high respectively. The climb up is a little strenuous, but once you have reached the top, you will be awed by fabulous views over Tasmania's mountains. The Frenchman's Cap Trail leads to another summit – to the Frenchman's Cap in the Franklin-Gordon Wild Rivers National Park.

Nature lovers will enjoy the beautiful South Coast and Port Davey Tracks which lead right through spectacular Southwest National Park for miles and miles. As there are no access roads to Melaleuca, the starting point of the tracks, hikers need to fly in, arrive by boat or hike here. Thousands of wilderness enthusiasts do so every year. Southwest is the largest national park in Tasmania and contains the southern part of the Tasmanian Wilderness World Heritage Area. With its temperate rainforests, the mountains of the Frankland Range and the Arthur Range, this refuge of 6,050 square kilometers (approx. 2,335 square miles) is one of the last unspoiled nature reserves on Earth.

at all. They simply could not pay the costs for the trip back by ship, so most of them stayed "down under". Charles Darwin, who started to develop his famous evolution theory about the origin of the species, was very interested in the situation of the prisoners in the Australian colony. He questioned any moral improvement of criminal elements by such a punishment or any other success, apart from the fact that the possibility of being carted off to a prisoners' colony at the other end of the world would probably have a certain deterrent effect. He left no doubt about the real sense behind the so-called iron gangs, the prisoners in chains. He described certain scenes, which he had experienced himself, vividly, including the prisoners slogging away under the supervision of guards with loaded rifles. "The power which the government possesses, by means of forced labour, of at once opening good roads throughout the country, has been, I believe, one main cause of the early prosperity of this colony."

When the mist and the first rays of sun create a romantic atmosphere over the bay, this gruesome piece of history seems tangible. The "Commandant's House", "The Church", "The Guard Tower" and "The Hospital" rise proudly between the mighty trees of the well-kept park. Walkways lead through the "Penitentiary" and allow you to look down into the single cells, only two cubic meters large (70.63 cubic feet), where the iron rings which the prisoners were chained to are still mounted on the meter-thick walls. It must have been a bizarre fate to be deported from the dark England of the 19th century and to end up in one of the loveliest landscapes in the world, as a convict. The view through the barred cell windows was a view of paradise. Inside it was sheer hell: isolated imprisonment, heavy beatings, prisoners vegetating away in chains; Port Arthur was the most gruesome of all Australian prisoner colonies. Over 2,000 prisoners died from the consequences of the inhuman prison conditions. Numerous graves on the Isle of the Dead just off the coast bear silent testimony to those times. With so much history it is quite possible that the ghost of Abel Janszoon Tasman might appear for a moment. He was the man who discovered Tasmania in 1642 and called it "Van Diemen's Land" after the Dutch governor of Java. Over one hundred years later, James Cook arrived at the same spot. A German, Heinrich Zimmermann, was with him who published his adventures in 1781 with the title: "Reise um die Welt mit Captain Cook"(Journey around the world with Captain Cook). He was probably the first German to set foot on Tasmania.

On Freycinet Peninsula you will find one the most beautiful national parks. It is a "must" for ornithologists and for those into beach flora and pristine beaches. The names of its bays are appropriate: Bluestone Bay, Honeymoon Bay, Sleepy Bay and Wineglass Bay. The Tasman Highway extends from the picturesque holiday

Sorell Peninsula on the Tasman Peninsula offers rural bliss (left page). According to Farmer Ian Dickinson from Blessington, he could not run his sheep station without first class sheep dogs (this page).

resort Coles Bay to St. Helen's on the east coast. Looking towards the hinterland you will get an unearthly panoramic view of gentle hills, grazing sheep on juicy green pastures, with jagged mountain ranges as an almost surreal backdrop. Along the shores of the ocean you will spot colorful fishing boats, elegant yachts and screeching seagulls between rocky bays and wide sandy beaches. With its 90,000 inhabitants, Launceston is Tasmania's third largest city. It lies on the Tamar River which runs its course as

"The Penitentiary" in Port Arthur seems idyllic today, but used to be one of the worst prisoner colonies of the British Empire (left). – Today the well-kempt parks surrounding the old prison buildings are a nice place to have a picnic (below).

broad as a lake and soon pours into the Bass Strait. Characteristic features of the "Garden City of the North", as Launceston sees itself, are extensive parks, churches reminiscent of southern England as well as splendid facades of Victorian merchant houses. The clock tower of the Royal Post Office, which was presented to Launceston at its centenary by King Edward XII, is a historic jewel. Just outside of town you will find a natural wonder: bizarre "Cataract Gorge", a canyon which was formed over thousands of years by the water masses of the Tamar. If you are not too sure about walking across the suspension bridge downriver, you can glide over the roaring water in a chair lift. Here, in the Tamar Valley, is the place where Tasmania's grapes grow, too. The coldest wine growing region in Australia produces excellent Rieslings, Chardonnays and Pinot Noirs in over one hundred vineyards. Connoisseurs drift from one winery to the next to taste these beauties.

The "Tassies" claim that of their seventeen national parks, three are the most beautiful in the world. There is no doubt that Tasmania's wilderness is one of the last reserves on Earth. A person who recognized this more than 100 years ago was Gustav Weindorfer. When this Austrian arrived in Tasmania, he was immediately smitten by its pristine mountain landscapes. Whilst the locals considered him an oddball, this immigrant built a wooden refuge for himself in the mountains of the Cradle Mountain

Visitors to the region who enjoy some comfort, even in the midst of the wilderness, relax around the open fireplace of the Cradle Mountain Lodge, which is not far from Weindorfer's simple wooden chalets and his grave. In winter the high plateau, which is not only home to Cradle Mountain Lake St. Clair National Park, but also to the adjoining Walls of Jerusalem National Park, and which covers more than half of the total island area, is covered in a deep, soft blanket of snow. In the summer months, between

region, which were completely inaccessible then. "This is my Waldheim, where there is no time and nothing matters." Visitors read this while they revel in the homely atmosphere of his lush garden. Weindorfer's rustic face looks at you from its memorial plaque in a way as though he were still alive somewhere around here. Weindorfer was long dead when the Cradle Mountain Lake St. Clair National Park was finally given its current status, something which Weindorfer had been supporting throughout his life.

Almost like it used to be: this nostalgic grocery store in Evandale is worth a visit, not only for the romantically inclined. But there is a sign of the times: "credit cards welcome" (above). Another bit of nostalgia: in Tasmania school kids wear uniforms (left).

One of the most beautiful nature experiences in Tasmania is to take a boat up the Gordon River (below). The sand dunes on Strahan's Ocean Beach with flowering dune plants (left).

November and April, the countless water bodies, ponds, mountain lakes – including the Great Lake, the highest lake in Australia – render hikes an unforgettable experience. With a bit of luck you might see a pretty possum or a quoll, the native wild cats with a pouch. And maybe you might even catch a glimpse of the notorious Tasmanian Devil. If you do, you can consider yourself fortunate. Foxes have been introduced from Europe specifically to decimate its population. The Tasmanian Devil is an aggressive, carnivorous marsupial which emanates "devilish" growls, according to the first settlers. When cornered it snarls threateningly.

Historic mining towns lie along the way to the coast. Zeehan used to be the third largest town in Tasmania around 1900, at the time of the silver rush. Today it has put historic steam engines from its mining days back onto the tracks. The "Abt Steam Railway" rumbles through rugged mountains and dense forests to the sea at Strahan. This small town with its 400 inhabitants in the bay of Macquarie Harbour has the only harbor along Tasmania's west coast. As the picturesque bay is largely blocked by a sand bank, bigger ships cannot enter. This is very fortunate for the picturesque idyll of this tiny pioneer town. In the past, mainly Queenstown's copper arrived here on mine trains and was loaded onto ships. You can hear the Indian Ocean roaring beyond the protective bay, giant waves crashing onto the shore. Broad beaches extend right to the horizon where they disappear in a fog of spray. Masses of sand, which has been blown into huge dunes, turn this rough coast almost into a desert. From here you can take a seaplane or a boat up the Gordon River into the archaic landscapes of the Franklin-Gordon Wild Rivers National Park. You can have a look at this piece of paradise, but you will not be able to visit the true depths of the Tasmanian wilderness. The distant ancient forests which have no road access remain reserved for nature.

At Eaglehawk Neck you will find the "Tessellated Pavement" which looks as though it had been laid by man (right). The cliffs on Diamond Island also have interesting structures (above).

It is beautifully lush at the
Russel Falls in Mount Field
National Park (above). – Lake
Wombat is one of the moraine
lakes in the Cradle Mountain
Lake St. Clair National Park
(right). – Stanley, on the foot
of the "table mountain" The
Nun, was founded in 1826 as
the headquarters of the Van
Diemen's Land Company
(following double page).

SILVER LINING ON THE HORIZON

AUSTRALIA'S MOST BEAUTIFUL TRAIN JOURNEYS

A train journey right across the Australian continent is an amazing experience. Several passengers lugging their backpacks still hurriedly make their way through the train station in Perth to catch the "Indian Pacific" to Sydney, whilst the eagle just looks on calmly as though he were them: are you ready for one of the most spectacular train journeys in the world? The majestic wedge-tail eagle is the symbol of the "Indian Pacific". This train with its silver wagons and diesel engine races from the Indian to the Pacific Ocean, as its name suggests, in 65 hours. It covers a distance of precisely 4,352 kilometers (2,704 miles), with an average speed of 67 kilometers (41 miles) per hour. This does not make the "Indian Pacific" one of the fastest trains in the world, but it is certainly one of the most spectacular ones. It holds a world record which is hard to break, unless the Australians have the ambition to be entered in the Guinness World of Records yet again and construct a railway racing track of 500 meters in length somewhere in the outback. Already today they have the longest dead straight stretch of railway between Nurina and Ooldea across the Nullarbor Plain, a length of 478 kilometers (297 miles). The passengers spend three nights in the "Indian Pacific", in more or less comfortable cabins, on their way between the two oceans. They cross different time and climatic zones and travel through landscapes with lush green fields, mountain regions, such as the Blue Mountains and long stretches of desert-like areas which the train cuts through like a flash of lighting in the midday sun. Along this route from west to east there are proper cities including Perth, Adelaide and Sydney, sleepy little towns, such as Cook, and gold mining towns, such as Kalgoorlie and Broken Hill. The

"The Ghan" (left) crosses the continent from north to south. – Just sparse shrubs: the "Indian Pacific" steams across the Nullarbor Plain (large photograph). – High-tech cockpit: train drivers in the "Indian Pacific" (above). – Camel drivers with beards: train drivers of the "Ghan" in Afghani look (right page, top). The Central Train Station in Sydney (right).

galleries. Broken Hill has become the last stop of their dreams for many artists. And between all these stops you spend your time looking out of the window, eating, drinking and chatting to your fellow passengers. Whether you are traveling first class with the Gold Kangaroo Service, the Red Kangaroo or in a sleeping chair, whether you have your own shower or share the communal one, the dining wagon and bars are the meeting point for everybody. This is the place where one half of the passengers – Australians who want to get to know their country once without a car or a plane – meet tourists from all over the world. When finally the sun rises over the Blue Mountains and Sydney comes close, many passengers start to feel sad. Why should one disembark after having crossed the continent, met lovely people and seen breathtaking landscapes? The trip itself is the aim of the "Indian Pacific", that is what makes it so very luxurious.

The red heart, the Australian outback, is considered the most hostile region on our planet. So it is no wonder that it was always a great dream to conquer these vast plains, this seemingly overpowering environment. It took a long time, but finally the Australian pioneering

Off Train Tours, which are appreciated by the passengers, usually take an hour and make a change from just staring out of the window. Gold dust of its heyday long gone still blows around Kalgoorlie. The wonderful old pubs and Hay Street with the "Ladies of the Night" do not help to change this feeling either. Unfortunately there is just enough time to enjoy a cold beer here before the train leaves the station again. In Cook, on the edge of the Nullarbor Plain, you get the chance to stretch your legs. In Adelaide you get whisked off on a quick city tour and in Broken Hill, the first or last station in New South Wales depending on where the trip started, there is just enough time to get a first impression of the silver mining history and to visit one of the numerous

spirit succeeded. Since February 2004, people have been able to travel from Adelaide on the south coast to Darwin on the north coast aboard the "Ghan". As early as 1870 there were first visions of a transcontinental north-south railway track. At the turn of the century, part of the northern stretches up to Pine Creek was completed. In the south one got as far as Oodnadatta. Finally, on August 4, 1929 Alice Spring was reached, the end of the line for many centuries. Only the legendary Afghan camel drivers with their skills and sense of orientation made the construction of the railway line along the old caravan routes possible. They lent the train its name: "The Ghan" is the abbreviation for Afghan. The front of the train looks like a camel, too, while the interior of the train suits the taste of the mature passengers. So it took all of seventy-five years to make the

dream come true. The whole stretch from the South Australian capital Adelaide via Port Augusta, Coober Pedy, through the red deserts of the outback, via Alice Springs, Tennant Creek and Katherine right up to the tropical north has a length of 2,979 kilometers (1,851 miles). The passengers spend a total of 47 hours, including two nights, in the silver wagons, the sleeping cabins, restaurants and lounges. They can disembark halfway, in Alice. During the four-hour stop they can visit the Desert Wildlife Park or disrupt their train ride for a flight or a bus tour to Uluru. This world-famous sacred site of the Aborigines is such an impressive natural won-

der that you simply have to see Ayers Rock if you happen to be traveling nearby. A trip to 25 million year-old Katherine Gorge with a helicopter or a boat is spectacular, too. The last part of the train ride on the approach to Darwin stands in complete contrast to the endless, red brown plains of central Australia. Everything is lush, green and steaming. Salt-water crocodiles, 6 meters (20 feet) in length, dozing on the banks of the rivers, take no notice of the "Ghan". The train itself did not take much notice of the kangaroos and camels along the way which have turned into a problem. At some point in time the Afghans disappeared, leaving their camels behind. As soon as they had been left by their masters, all the camels could do was reproduce. And their reproduction rate was so high that they now move through the red outback in their thousands and are occasionally run over by the "Ghan".

Apart from these two transcontinental showpieces, "Rail Australia" has further treasures

on rails which all have one thing in common: they teach you to see. Unfortunately the service of the luxurious "Great South Pacific Express", which ran along the east coast from Sydney to Cairns via Brisbane, was temporarily disrupted in 2004. But the "Sunlander" and the "Queenslander", which both commute between Brisbane and Cairns, also hold special travel experiences in store. The same applies to the nostalgic trains "Savannahlander", which connect Cairns and Forsayth, and the "Gulflander", which runs from Croydon to Normanton, or the "Spirit of the Outback", which you can catch from Brisbane to Longreach. And what do these lovely trains teach you to see? First of all you relax while the huge expanse of the country rolls past outside. Then a flood of real, authentic landscape pictures spreads out right in front of your eyes. And then you start to watch, you are amazed, you stop talking and start to see everything afresh.

In the outback, such as in Kuranda, or on the platforms in the city: passengers are treated courteously (left page). – Stylish wagons, including an elegant dining wagon, and correctly dressed staff are part of this special treatment (large photograph, left). – Nostalgia pure: into the east, following the camels (above).

Wine-growing (above), opal diggers (center) and bizarre rock formations, including the Remarkable Rocks in Flinders Chase National Park (below) are just as typical for South Australia as the seemingly endless wheat fields (right page).

SOUTH AUSTRALIA

ADELAIDE
BAROSSA VALLEY
FLINDERS RANGES
KANGAROO ISLAND
COOBER PEDY

South Australia is the most important wine region in the country. It is even more important than New South Wales. The huge vineyards of McLaren Vale are not even amongst the largest.

Australia offers freedom to humans and animals, including this sea lion. Landscapes, such as those of Mount Remarkable National Park (center), are impressive symbols of this freedom.

South Australia is the great unknown of the "fifth continent". Although it has many treasures:
from vineyards in green valleys to opal mining in the dusty outback,
from Adelaide's diverse leisure time facilities to unique Kangaroo Island.

South Australia is not the geographical term for the south coast of the "fifth" continent, which starts more or less around Melbourne (in Victoria) and ends in Perth (Western Australia). Only the middle part, with a coastline of 3,700 kilometers (2,300 miles), belongs to the Federal State of South Australia. It is the only state which borders on all other mainland states, apart from Canberra's Australian Capital Territory. But it is not only the name of the state that can be a little misleading. Almost every second bottle of Australian wine comes from South Australia. S.A., as this state is called for short, produces more than half of all Australian wines. Consequently many people envision South Australia as having fertile soils and not the desert-like outback that people know from the Northern Territory. But in fact 80 percent of the total area of South Australia is outback. Not even 1 percent of the state's population lives here. Another thing that almost nobody knows or even guesses: South Australia is the driest state of the driest continent on Earth. But on the other hand it is culturally the most European influenced state next to Tasmania. British, Greek, Italian and also German influences are dominant. The Barossa Valley, for example, is a German domain. These few examples already demonstrate that this state really is the large unknown with a bounty of interesting things in store, waiting to be discovered.

1.5 million people live in the total state area of just under one million square kilometers (around 385,000 square miles), pre-cisely 12.8 percent of Australia. Three quarters of them live in and around Adelaide. Aside from this city of a million, there are merely a few smaller towns, amongst which Whyalla and Mount Gambier are the largest, with over 20,000 inhabitants. Murray Bridge, Port Augusta and Port Lincoln only have 10,000 to 20,000 inhabitants.

The scope of landscapes includes wide desert plains with salt lakes in the north, which partially lie below sea level, and steep coastal cliffs in the south. There is fertile land and regions rich in mineral resources, such as opals, gold, silver, coal, oil, gas, iron, copper, lead, zinc or uranium. To this day the Olympic Dam Mine in the north is one of the largest copper-uranium-gold-silver mines in the world. The Murray River is the main watercourse, meandering through the country over a length of 640 kilometers (approx. 400 miles), with paddle wheel steamers and houseboats chugging around on it. The Murray River spills into the sea near Adelaide.

South Australia is also called the "Festival State". This is due to its capital and maybe also due to something rather curious. As Melbourne's little rival, Adelaide mixes a busy lifestyle with a relaxed cultural program, which tries to measure up a little to Sydney's. It is no coincidence that the modern Festival Centre with its tent roof looks a little like Sydney's Opera House. The cultural center includes several theaters and stages and is also the venue of the nationally known "Art Festival" with theater, opera, ballet and exhibitions. The South Australia Museum complements this rich cultural spectrum with its collection of Aboriginal art. However, the Tandanya Aboriginal Cultural Centre, where you can also

The Remarkable Rocks on Kangaroo Island (left page), where 30,000 kangaroos live (above), look like sculptures.

see and experience contemporary Aboriginal art and culture, is even more authentic. In S.A. people are very proud of their museums, galleries and festivals, but also of their shopping malls, sidewalk cafés and restaurants. Glenelg, which is only a tram ride away, has lovely beaches right on the Gulf of St. Vincent.

The surroundings of the capital are worth a visit, too. The aforementioned Barossa Valley lies around 50 kilometers (30 miles)

South Australia proudly calls itself "Festival State". In Adelaide everything is cheerful and colorful – the sculptures in front of the Parliament (left), or a mural on Rundle Street (below).

northeast of the capital. This is Australia's most famous wine growing region with numerous winegrowers and settlements of German origin, which were founded in the mid-19th century. The influence of German culture can be clearly seen in the architecture and the lifestyle. You can find German bread and cuisine. Particularly in Tanunda, called Langmeil up to World War I, there are numerous German roots. And German names dominate the gravestones. One of them is August Klavel, the pastor who led a German community to Langmeil.

The Eyre Peninsula lies west of Adelaide. It has a variety of landscapes, from craggy rock formations, protected bays, mighty cliffs and limestone caves to the dusty desert of the Nullarbor Plain. Half of the region consists of nature conservation areas and unspoiled wilderness. In Port Augusta you will come across a base for the "School of the Air" and for the "Royal Flying Doctor Service" to cater for this region with its huge areas with almost no human population. Along the coast you can go whale-watching throughout the year. It is almost impossible not to see one of these giant mammals during the period of June to September, their breeding season.

On the way to Fleurieu Peninsula you will come across Hahndorf. It is a very German place which was founded by East Prussia in 1839. It even holds the typical "Schützenfeste" and here you still find houses built in the alpine style. The Fleurieu Peninsula starts a few kilometers south of Adelaide and is a holiday region, offering the full range of water sports, including surfing, scuba diving and fishing. However, the continuation of this headland is even more exciting: Kangaroo Island.

In some parts of Australia kangaroos are almost a plague. Tourists, who also come to Australia to see this animal, find this

look for something to eat. Fenced-in picnic spots have been set up so that the tourists can enjoy their lunch without being bothered by the kangaroos. Here, the people sit in the cage – not the other way around. The marsupials watch wide-eyed to see what the humans do and what they eat behind their wire netting.

Kangaroos, after whom this third largest island of Australia is named, are a constant cause of conflict between conservationists

hard to believe, as they don't get to see very many of them during the day. That is unless they visit Kangaroo Island, around 120 kilometers (75 miles) southwest of Adelaide. There is a ferry connection from the capital to the island.

If you want to experience kangaroos – and koalas, too – in their natural environment, you should definitely catch a ferry across. It is worth it! The nervous animals, which are active at night and usually so shy, are not afraid of humans on their island, as they have never experienced them as enemies here. As they are fed by the visitors, some of the "roos", as the Australians call them, get so cheeky that they boldly rummage around bags and rucksacks to

Adelaide is a young, lively city of a million people, even though it may seem a little reserved at first in its Victorian attire (top). – This first impression might also be supported by the time-honored main building of the university, opposite Central Station, right in the center of town (left).

The other South Australia is that of the endless plains. This is what the Strzelecki Track looks like (both photos) Following double page: Lake Eyre, a saltlake.

and hunters. Most farmers consider this animal a plague which eats away the grass and thus deprives their sheep and cattle of fodder. At the same time conservationists warn that the state kill quota of five million kangaroos every year could lead to the extinction of these very unique animals.

At the moment, around 30,000 kangaroos of all different sizes from 35 centimeters to almost two meters – hop around on this island which is 145 by 40 kilometers (90 by 25 miles) in size. There are a total of ninety-three different species of kangaroos and their close relatives. You just have to keep an eye out for the mothers when they have little ones, commonly referred to as Joeys. She can give a hard kick with her muscular and clawed back legs. But before that happens, she issues a warning to Joey by thumping the ground with her feet. This is the signal for it to quickly hop into the mother's pouch – to safety. Contrary to widespread opinion, you can usually only see a Joey's paws sticking out of the pouch and not its head.

But let's travel to the other 80 percent of South Australia, to the endless outback. After all, Stuart Highway, which connects Adelaide with Darwin in the extreme north of Australia, is also called Explorer Highway. Our first destination off the highway is the Flinders Ranges. This fascinating mountain range, with its changing colors and bizarre shapes, even offers a trip to the Great Wall of China: here this name refers to a distinctive mountain ridge, built up like a wall.

Wilpena, oasis and centre of the Flinders Range National Park, is embedded in lush green. The Aborigines who live here call themselves the people from the rocky hills. Ancient rock drawings from the Adnayamathanha are hidden in Chambers Gorge in the north of Flinders Range National Park.

The highlight for any tourist in the Flinders Ranges is the Wilpena Pound, a broad basin surrounded by steep cliffs. You get the best view of it from St. Mary's Peak, the highest summit of the mountain range, around 1,200 meters high.

See page 143

This adventurer near Glendambo is "on the road" in the mud. – This road sign on Kangaroo Island warns about echidnas crossing. – The mechanics shop in Coober Pedy, a tour in the Flinders Ranges National Park, a visit to an opal digger and his mates in the pub, battered road signs and strange Bluey Blundstone's Blacksmith Shop in Melrose are further treats that you can almost only experience with your own car. If you hope for a bus or a train, you will never get to these remote destinations in South Australia (clockwise from top left).

NO DISTANCE TOO FAR

THE ROYAL FLYING DOCTOR SERVICE

The history of medical care in the Australian outback, before the "Royal Flying Doctor Service" was founded, sounded adventurous. This is an anecdote from the period prior to 1928: Postmaster Tuckett of Halls Creek had to perform an operation on Jimmy Darcy, who had suffered serious internal

injuries after falling from his horse, without any surgical instruments, disinfectants and anesthetics. The only guidance Tuckett had were medical instructions which he received via the Morse telegraph of his post station. If need be, Tuckett would just have to use his pen knife and a few razor blades, according to Dr.Holland's instructions from the west Australian city of Perth. In any case Darcy would die without an operation.

Thus the post and telegraph master set to work under the light of a petroleum lamp. Sweating nervously he followed the surgical instructions, which the doctor was cabling to him over the endless distances of the northwest of

Australia right into his headphones – step by step. After the operation was completed, the doctor made his way to the patient himself. It took him six days onboard a boat for cattle transport to travel up the west coast. In the port town of Derby he grabbed a car and continued eastbound. Unfortunately it broke down

several times en route on the gravel and dirt tracks. Then he hitched a ride on a horse-drawn carriage for the last part of his trip. When he finally arrived in Halls Creek, Darcy was dead.

That was how things were at the time. Nowadays the twin-engine airplanes reach remote cattle or sheep stations quite quickly, if medical help is needed. After the plane has landed and the red dust has settled, each step is quick routine. On the flight back to the "Base Hospital" the patient is already hooked up to a drip and is supplied with oxygen, while the accompanying doctor discusses his diagnosis via radio with his medical colleagues. At the home

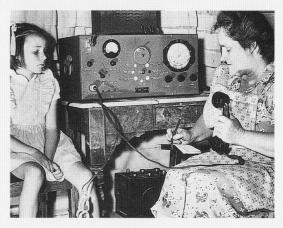

An aircraft is always on standby (above left). –
Office in Kalgoorlie (top right page). Control station
of the Central Section in Alice Springs (large photograph). – Patients radioing the Flying Doctor (above).
– Patient's stretcher in the airplane (right).

140

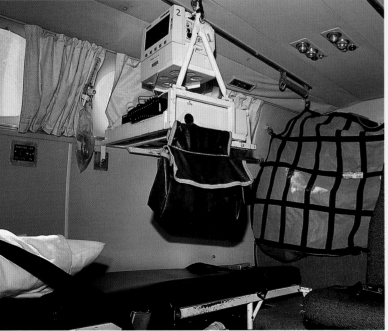

The Flying Doctor Service was founded thanks to Reverend John Flynn. This Presbyterian priest caused a huge outcry when he deliberately fed Jimmy Darcy's story to the press. Inspired by the progresses in aviation, he was obsessed by the idea of supplying the people of the huge Australian outback, who lived in constant fear of diseases and accidents, with medical care by airplane. In 1928 his idea suddenly started to take shape when an electrical engineer of German descent from Adelaide, a certain Alfred Träger, invented a simple pedal wireless. Now communication was secured. Soon Dr. Vincent Welch, the first flying doctor, and his pilot, Arthur Affleck, took off on their first job for the new "Aerial Medical Service" of the Presbyterian Inland Mission. Within a year Welch and Affleck had covered a distance of 20,000 kilometers (around 12,450 miles) on fifty flights, had consulted hundreds of patients and had visited dozens of country doctors' surgeries.

Soon Träger's pedal wireless was replaced by twelve-volt batteries – nowadays thousands of radio telephones run on the frequency of the flying doctors. With the blessing of the Queen, the "Aerial Medical Service" turned into the "Royal Doctor's Service" in 1955. Today it completes over 30,000 flight missions and telephone consultations a year and attends to more than 200,000 patients.

airport the ambulance is ready and waiting to take the patient directly to the operating room, if required. Such an emergency operation is not always necessary. First the doctor and the patient orient themselves by telephone with the help of an anatomical map on which all body parts are clearly marked by letters and numbers. If the doctor, who is often hundreds of kilometers away, recognizes the medical problem, local treatment with the so-called Bush Pharmacy, a standardized chest of drugs, is undertaken. If that does not help, the doctor will fly to the patient for a personal consultation. In the worst case, the patient is then transported to a clinic at the "Flying Doctor Base".

141

Even further out and further north, where the heat sizzles and the road trains – the trucks of sometimes more than 50 meters (164 feet) in length with several trailers – are the true kings of the highway, you should definitely not miss out the opal digger town, Coober Pedy. It makes a nice break to the monotony of the outback. Of course this town is as dusty as the surrounding desert, but it is also as surreal as a sci-fi movie and as strange as its inhabitants, who drink more beer than water. There is even a keg of beer on one of the graves in the cemetery. It bears the following wise words: "Have a drink on me."

On the other hand Coober Pedy is also typically Australian, in that you must have a very good reason to found a settlement in this Never-Never Land, or else you have to find one. The raison d'être for Coober Pedy is opals. In 1911 this rare mineral with its colors of the rainbow was discovered in this very place. Every day more than 3,000 people of all different nationalities dig around in this moon landscape. By the way, Coober Pedy means "white man in a hole" in the language of the Aborigines. Life mostly runs its course underground. And not only during working hours: many of the dwellings are dugouts, caves blasted out from the rock, furnished like

The Mungerannie Oasis along the Birdsville Track is a little paradise (left page). – Innamincka Reserve: spoonbills waiting for prey (below), a Western Corella spreading its wings.

normal living rooms and bedrooms. Only underground is it bearable; here people can escape from the heat. Even the churches and a hotel have gone underground. And the golf course is brown here. Lush green has not got a chance in this place.

Any visit to Coober Pedy is incomplete without having seen the mine shafts where machinery eats into the soft rock and spits it out above ground. These earth movements create the countless, cone-shaped earth mounds in this strange place. It looks as though giant moles have been digging their burrows here. If you do not fancy a look at the mines, you should at least ask for directions to Salt 'n' Pepper, a place a few kilometers outside of Coober Pedy. Here the land abruptly breaks off, colorful layers of rock are exposed and shine in the setting sun as though it were the largest jewelry store in the world. In the evening falcons patrol the skies over this curious endlessness. It is so still and quiet, it is breathtaking. And the natural beauty of the place touches any visitor to the core.

There is just one thing that remains to be resolved: what is this weird thing that makes South Australia the Festival State, aside from Adelaide's cultural and leisure activities? It is the Curdimurka Outback Ball. Every two years the desert comes alive, dances and shakes. 4,000 "Aussies", dressed in tuxedo and evening dress, meet up at the Old Ghan train station of Curdimurka, more than 700 kilometers (435 miles) from Adelaide, to enjoy the largest open-air ball on the continent. They arrive by car, in busses, on motorbikes or with their own plane. Despite the enormous heat and the bothersome flies, the red-brown ground turns into a shining parquet. Of course Curdimurka is not Cannes and the outback is not the Côte d'Azur, but the vibes are great! Instead of waltzes, there is country music and instead of polished dance shoes, cowboy boots with spurs are worn with the tuxedo. But best of all is the ballroom by night: covered by a huge dark blue canopy with stars that shine brighter than anywhere else on Earth.

The Bearded Dragon Lizard
(above) and the red dunes
of the Strzelecki desert
(right) give South Australia
a primeval feel.

Eucalyptus trees, such as those along
Wilpena Creek (above) or the
Bunyeroo Valley (right) render the
Flinders Ranges National Park a
"must" on any tour of South Australia
– at least for hikers who can climb
summits of 1,100 meters (3,608 feet)
height here.

Following double page:
bird's eye view of an opal field.

A PIECE OF THE RAINBOW

WITH THE OPAL DIGGERS IN THE OUTBACK

The opal fields of Australia lie in the Artesian Basin which is over two million square kilometers (772,200 square miles) large and which extends over the states of South Australia,

wind instrument of the Aborigines. The opal shimmers in the whole spectrum of colors and the Aborigines believe that a rainbow originally put the color into this stone. And this is

New South Wales and Queensland. The opal's character changes from field to field and each opal finds a lover. But particularly the fields of Lightning Ridge produce a true rarity: the black opal. Its fiery play of colors is enhanced by the natural deep black color of the stone's body. Such a "red on black" is the dream of any miner. It fetches several thousand dollars per carat, even right here on the mining field.

The opal is the national gem of Australia. Around 95 percent of all opals on the world market come from "down under". If you want to take a truly Australian souvenir back home with you, then you have to bring back this fantastic gemstone, aside from a didgeridoo, the

precisely what you hold in your hand in awe: a piece of the rainbow.

The first part of our trip takes us across the Great Dividing Range. The Warrumbungles, the "Crooked Mountains", 500 kilometers (310 miles) northwest of Sydney, are our first destination. They lie on the western edge of the Great Dividing Range and were formed through volcanic activity approximately 13 million years ago. The bizarre rock towers, battlements and domes, which were formed by erosion, attract hikers throughout the year. And in between these rocks there are almost endless purple fields. This purple weed, called Peterson's Curse, is lovely to look at, but the

farmers hate it, as it is poisonous to their cattle. They lose hundreds of animals every year because of it.

We continue northwest on compacted dust and gravel tracks. On our way to Lightning Ridge

The people of Coober Pedy live in their cozily furnished and decorated dugouts which give them shelter from the unbearable heat (left). – There are a variety of opals, aside from black, fire and crystal opals: this is a boulder opal (large photograph). – Opal store in Coober Pedy (center right) and jewelry from Cairns (bottom right) and New South Wales: designer Barbara Gasch with an opal necklace (above right).

mark. Several thousand people live in Lightning Ridge, but very few are registered. This is pretty unique in Australia.

An opal dealer, who I met on my travels through Australia, has good connections to Lightning Ridge. She kindly gave me a few phone numbers and the first person I called said: "No worries mate". Next day, Marc picked us up from our campsite and we drove out to the mine fields together. They all lie outside of town and have the characteristic earth mounds next to the mining shafts. The place looks like a crater landscape. The shaft of Marc's mine is 15 meters (49 feet) deep.

Around Lightning Ridge, opals are found at depths of up to 30 meters (100 feet) in the clay rock. They are found in layers or as nobbies – round clumps. The miners usually work on their own or in small teams. They dig subterranean passages; you will hardly find open pits here. The old-timers still had to slave away by candlelight using a pickax and shovel. At least Marc uses a pneumatic drill and an electric

we keep on coming across emu families – the father with his four to twelve chicks. After the chicks have hatched, the mother gets up and leaves and the father is left to rear the chicks. Although these flightless birds stop in their tracks to watch the cars drive by, they run away immediately if you stop.

Approximately 400 kilometers (250 miles) northwest of Warrumbungles National Park, in the middle of the outback on the border to Queensland, we eventually arrive in the opal mining town Lightning Ridge – a hot, unspectacular place. We are welcomed by a sign, telling us that this is Lightning Ridge; its number of inhabitants is indicated by a question

151

conveyor system. Often excavators and electric front hoes are employed, too. Marc considers Australia's opal fields a large casino. The investments are often high and you rarely win. The most varied people come together here. Retirees, families, bachelors, adventurers and people looking for an alternative lifestyle. Sometimes tourists arrive and never leave. But there are also those who have no place anymore in another society, long-term unemployed, losers, loners, eccentrics, alcoholics,

criminals. Nobody gives their family name. And if you were to ask for a Mr. So-and-So, you would just get a shrug for an answer. But you can find a Little Joe, Big John, Aeroplane Jo, Stinky Steve, Goldtooth Jim and Redbeard. These guys usually get their nicknames from certain events or from certain personal characteristics.

Those who are not only looking for quick wealth, but who like the lifestyle, stay on longest. But also those who have not got a chance anymore to find a job elsewhere. It is a colorful mix of forty different nationalities, only few are Australian. This multicultural cocktail creates an interesting atmosphere, but the various groups also like to keep to themselves. The Germans here are more German than in Germany, the Greeks are more Greek and the conflict between the Serbs and Croats is even felt on these faraway opal fields.

Marc grinds, polishes and cuts the stones of other opal diggers. That way the stones fetch a better price with the dealers, who come to this place from all over the world, as they can now recognize the colors in the stone. Others sell their opals raw, in jam jars, to dealers such as Mike, who have to have a good idea as to what can be cut out of the raw stone. We visit Mike in a darkened motel room. Every six weeks he and his partner take the tough trip upon themselves to come to this godforsaken place, as he has become enamored with the black opals from Lightning Ridge.

Next day Marc's friend, Peter Richter, takes us into his mine. It has meanwhile become so large that it joins up with that of his neighbors.

at boarding school in the next largest town. There are those miners who have a regular job in nearby towns or on farms close by. These guys mine as a hobby. Others take on part-time work to finance their hunt for opals. Some of them have fled city life, others are hiding from the law. All of them want to live without rules and regulations and are fascinated by the freedom of the Australian outback. Some of them consider opal mining pure business, others are addicted to the beauty of this gem. Retirees have found a place where they can live cheaply, with a claim fee of only 150 Australian dollars a year, and where they keep fit at the same time. The younger ones aim at the large find, at the ultimate color kick. But they all have one thing in common. Deep down they are fortune hunters who have this dream of being rich – very, very rich – soon.

In the language of the Aborigines, Coober Pedy means "white man in hole": mining is hard work (above left), in the labyrinth of the galleries (left center). – Trial drilling with heavy equipment (large photograph). – The dealer checks the quality of the raw opals. – Magically shimmering colors are typical for the Australian opal (left).

Peter employs an excavator for digging. His wife, Trish, helps him and checks the freshly excavated places for opals. Peter's grandparents, the Richters, came from Germany. He arrived in Lightning Ridge ten years ago, on holiday with his family, and got stuck here. They lived in two old busses for the first ten years. Only three months before I turned up did they move into their corrugated iron house. It is built very high, due to the heat, and on one side you can open up a huge door. His boys continue to sleep in the bus when they are not

153

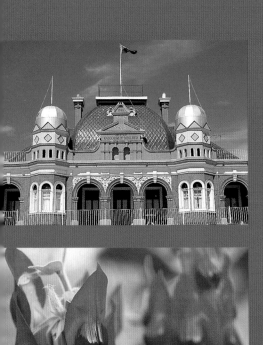

The Kalgoorlie Hotel (above).
Sturt's Desert Pea belongs to the
pea family (center). Giant karri
trees in Beedelup National Park
(below). – Wave Rock, located
between Coolgardie and Perth, is
made of granite (right).

WESTERN AUSTRALIA

PURNULULU NATIONAL PARK

KIMBERLEYS · SHARK BAY

KARIJINI NATIONAL PARK

FREEMANTLE · PERTH

Hundreds of bizarre stone columns,
"pinnacles", have developed in the
sandy desert of the Nambung
National Park north of Perth. They
come in various shapes and sizes.
The largest ones are around 4 meters
(13 feet) high.

Hikers in Stirling Range National Park (left). – The Kangaroo Paw (Anigozanthos manglesii) is the national flower of Western Australia (center). – Contrasts in Perth: colonial architecture and a modern skyline (right).

Perth, "The City of Lights" and the capital of Western Australia, governs a third of the "red continent". This State is a world of contrasts where you can find sharks, vineyards, crocodiles, deserts, colonial and glitzy high-rise architecture as well as idyllic coastal towns.

When the first Pallottine brothers of the Limburg order made their way to Naples to climb aboard the steamship "Friedrich der Große" on January 16, 1901, the extent of their adventure could not be fathomed. Neither by the Aborigines, who were living in the wild, approximately 2,500 kilometers (1,550 miles) from Perth, nor by Beagle Bay, the godforsaken place in the Indian Ocean which was to receive a gorgeous church, nor by the missionaries themselves who were going to spend the second half of their lives there. When these courageous monks from Germany were on firm ground again in Perth, which was still a provincial harbor town at the end of the world then, their first introduction to Australia were swarms of mosquitoes and cyclones. On top of that, their ship ran aground on their onward trip to Beagle Bay. But they faced their mission and a tough life bravely, including the chronic lack of water in the boiling hot bush, far away from the motherhouse. Today their freshly whitewashed, neo gothic Sacred Heart Church looks like a Fata Morgana in the red-brown wilderness. You will find German graves on the cemetery next to it. Visitors who step into this church, far away from any civilization, may experience a little of the glory of the Holy Spirit: thousands of artistically cut and polished cowrie shells and mother-of-pearl decorate the altar and the nave, 15,000 bricks, which the monks baked themselves, support a bell tower 12 meters high. The bell tower was completed in 1917 and the bells for it, as well as the old reed organ, were made by the German "Schiedmayer Pianoforte Factory Stuttgart". Led by Father Wilhelm Droste, the mission pioneers made the countless bricks and tiles themselves by hand, under the most primitive conditions. It seems unreal that just a few minutes flight away from this cozy mission church there should be a wilderness with very few options for any emergency landing. The Bucaneer Archipelago, with its countless ragged bays and mangrove swamps and more than 800 rocky islands, is very close to the mission. In the hinterland you find the sizzling hot, pancake-flat Australian outback which is sporadically crossed by watercourses where large crocodiles up to 6 meters (20 feet) in length lurk. A morbid fascination has developed around these huge reptiles since the American photo model Ginger Meadows fell victim to a saltwater crocodile at the Cascade Falls on Prince Regent River, Kimberley in 1987. The river became famous as a consequence of this tragedy. Today's Prince Regent Flora and Fauna Nature Reserve covers an area two and a half times the size of Rhode Island. It has the highest rate of precipitation in the whole of Western Australia and is one of the untouched wilderness areas on the continent. Visitors can only access the reserve by boat or by plane. The King's Cascade waterfalls of the Regent River are a highlight of the northern coastal regions, aside from the Python Cliffs, Mount Trafalgar, Pitta Gorge and the dense rain forests. You can cross the wide expanses of Australia's north on Australia's longest Adventure Drive: the Savannah Way. It runs from Broome to Cairns via Darwin and is signposted along a length of 3,500 kilometers (about 2,200 miles). Some 900 kilometers (560 miles) of it is dirt and gravel tracks.

Termite hills in Wittenoom Gorge in Karijini National Park (left page).
The girth of the boab trees in the Kimberleys is impressive.

The stretch from Beagle Bay to Broome is easy, if it has not just rained and if your car has a four-wheel drive and a long-range tank. And if the bumps and waves made by the road trains have been freshly leveled out by a grader. But it still remains an adventure: for miles and miles the vehicles move towards civilization across the red earth. Occasionally pick-up trucks drive past heavily, heading for the opposite direction. They are often full of cheerful Aborigines

Two helpers take a well-earned break while loading cattle for slaughter at Drysdale River Station. This station lies close to Gibb River Road which cuts right through the Kimberleys (left).

returning from their weekend shopping in Broome. You see a lot of empty Emu Red beer cans along the way. In the dark, these red cans, which contain 4.5 percent alcohol, shine like a beacon in the headlights. Because of them you cannot really get lost in the outback, the "Aussies" tell us jokingly. Broome has petrol stations and proper roads, supermarkets selling ice-cold beer, hotel pools, air conditioners and soft beds. Since the Pallottine brothers found their way here, this place in the middle of nowhere has become a popular holiday resort. When, at Cable Beach, which incidentally got its name from the subsea cable of the China Telegraph Company, the blood red sun dips into the sea, strange camel shadows are pro-

jected onto the wide sandy beach. The tourist attraction "Camel Ride at Sunset", which is similarly popular here as in the Arabian region, is responsible for them. In the background the Indian Ocean glitters, the bottle palms sway in the evening breeze, seagulls hover around the fish and chips stand and contented surfers tie their boards back onto their car roofs. The best way of getting a good perspective of this oasis of civilization is on a round trip with a Cessna. Hotel pools glow in turquoise-green colors between the race course and the Japanese cemetery. The flat endlessness, where dark storm clouds build up on the horizon in the evening, starts right behind the last buildings of this small town. Hundreds of reptiles hang out in water holes, as captured crocodiles are held right next to the Pearl Coast Zoo. They are kept behind very thin mesh wire, or so it may seem to the visitor when he or she takes a close look at these dangerous giants.

In 1880 Broome was populated by Malaysian, Japanese, European and Chinese pearl fishermen. Its fate seemed sealed when in 1935 the worst cyclone in its history completely flattened the place.

with modern civilization with their supplies, Broome is just a place to sleep and shower, with a petrol station selling kerosene for their planes and cold beer for themselves. Flying in the hinterland is often a real challenge, the bush pilots assure us proudly. There are often hundreds of miles without an airstrip or radio stations, but often extreme weather conditions. A single engine plane will drop 180 meters a minute when its engine breaks down, one

When the little town was built up again it was bombed by the Japanese in 1942, since Australia, as a member of the Commonwealth, stood on the side of the Allies. From 1950 onwards, the demand for pearls started to dwindle, as now only plastic buttons were sewed onto blouses and shirts worldwide. Fortunately for Broome, British Lord Alistair McAlpine, advisor for Margaret Thatcher and treasurer of the British Conservatives, discovered Cable Beach on a stopover and built the exclusive Cable Beach Club which attracted prosperous clients from then on.

But what is the value of all this compared to the adventures in the wild? For the bush pilots in any case, who link up the outback

Pure adventure: driving through the Pentecoast River and the Cockburn Range, Gibb River Road, Kimberleys (above). Pure outdoor romance: camp for the night at the Pentecoast River, Gibb River Road, Kimberleys. Nothing is more pleasant than when the cool night drives away the sizzling heat of the day (left).

The best way to see the strange rock formations of the Bungle Bungles in the Purnululu National Park is from a helicopter (left). – Gould's goanna can get up to 1.5 meters (5 feet) long (below).

of the guys who flew around Western Australia tells us. That often leaves you with only 15 minutes in the air. Bishop John Jobst, who was the last German bishop in Broome up until the mid 1990s, has many wild flight stories in store. For instance once he was trying to do a propeller start with his cassock blowing. The aircraft started and rolled over him, but then he just managed to grab its tail and hold on tight. To the horror of the tower crew the single engine plane rolled right across the runway, dragging the bishop behind it. Luckily it came to a stop in a bush. Apparently the nuns who were heaved out from the back seats fainted simultaneously. But these incidents did not bother this man. After he was ordained priest in 1950 and was then literally sent into the desert, this missionary had to drive thousands of kilometers every month in a four-by-four to visit his five missions and twenty outstations in an area of 773,000 square kilometers (around 298,000 square miles), double the size of his homeland, Germany.

The cross-country destinations could often not be reached for days if the bishop's expedition got stuck in the mud following heavy rains. This is why this ambitious man of God took a crash course to become a pilot in distant Perth. Then he flew to his flock himself.

The achievements of the Christian mission out in the bush remain controversial. The Australian Musical "Bran New Day", an Aboriginal production, was sold out for a long time after it had its premiere in Perth. It was broadcast by Australian TV and heated up long buried emotions about the issue of the indigenous people. The provoking stage play presented the church mission as being partially responsible for the identity crisis of the Aborigines and the sad demise of their values. However, the elders of these people point out that they would have been even worse off without the mission stations, where there was medical care, school education and access to modern Australian society. Today the

Termite hills (above). – A bird's eye view of Purnululu National Park (right). Eucalyptus trees around a billabong, Pilbara (following double page).

See page 169

WILDERNESS, VAST LANDSCAPES, ADVENTURE

A TRIP THROUGH THE KIMBERLEYS

The Kimberleys are truly still pure wilderness, without car parks and the whole leisure thing. Not as developed as other national parks, but therefore more natural, untouched and isolated, this is how the Crocodile Dundee from Broome, the crocodile farmer and filmmaker Malcolm Douglas, describes the last wilderness of Australia. In the Kimberleys

you will find places and landscapes that are so far away from civilization that you will feel as though you are on a different planet. Occasionally you will meet ranchers, such as Bluey, in this thinly populated vastness. Bluey is a typical rancher from this area, marked by life out here: clear blue eyes, the color of the sky, a handshake that almost breaks your bones, an iron will and smiling calm. No worries, Perth is thousands of miles away and it is a huge trip even to Broome or Darwin.

The Kimberleys extend around the northwestern tip of Western Australia and offer pure outback adventure. Impressive limestone gorges, intricate networks of caves and enormous tropical forests wait to be discovered, combined with evidence of the culture of the so-called Bradshaw Aboriginals which still cannot be

fully classified to this day. This region, which is three times the size of Great Britain, is one of the last continuous wilderness areas on this planet. It has an unbelievable diversity of landscapes, starting from high plateaus over deep gorges and river valleys to waterfalls and wild coasts. It is a very sparsely populated region. Only 28,000 people live in the small towns such as Kununarra in the northeast, Kalumburu in the north, Broome in the west and Halls Creek in the south. In between these towns there is the huge vastness of seemingly unpopulated land. But appearances are deceiving. Around 12,000 Aborigines live here and have claim over the land. If you plan to drive to farms and wilderness camps, you should obtain accurate and up-to-date information about the road and weather conditions, before you set off. Warning signs remind you to be careful. And you need to respect the Aboriginal culture and keep away from their sacred sites. And – beware – although freshwater crocodiles are not considered dangerous to humans, they are still definitely not cuddly toys.

Bluey has a serious problem: his 7-year-old son, Gregory, who is as cheeky as a playful kangaroo. Gregory is raised on Mornington Ranch, a bush

camp in the heart of the Kimberleys. It is a good base from which you can set off to discover the 3,000 square kilometers (1,160 square miles) of remote gorges and tropical savannas. Gregory could become a rancher, a cattle driver, ornithologist, rugby player, crocodile hunter or enter the tourism business, like his parents, Jay "Bluey" and Anna Cook. But what does he really, really want to do? He wants to become a pilot and when he informs you of this he looks you straight in the eye with as much determination as a saltwater crocodile fixating its prey. If you do not want to leave your parents and the

able to keep his 4,000 cattle. The bush camp belongs to the Australian Wildlife Conservancy (AWC) which saved it from the construction plans for a dam which was to supply Perth

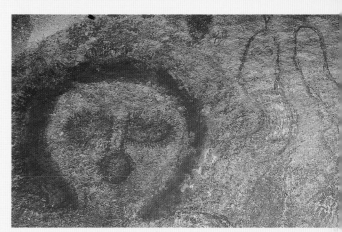

with water. But the meat prices have fallen, the amount of livestock is too large and the long transport is uneconomical. So Bluey will invest in amenities for soft tourism, including safari tents, too. Sitting around the campfire in the evening, waiting for the white owl to move into the huge eucalyptus tree for the night. And that is something you can experience without the Internet or a pilot's license.

wilderness early on, training as a pilot in the middle of the outback is a problem. Luckily Gregory still has time and Bluey can see light at the end of the tunnel, as the government has decided to finance a PC with Internet access for each school kid in the outback. That and the "School of the Air", which supplies Gregory with half an hour of education every day, must do. Whether you consider it progress or a curse, globalization will soon even affect the most hidden parts of the Kimberleys. Bluey pulls his black rancher hut down over his eyes even further. God knows whether he will be

Faces of the outback: Malcolm Douglas (left page, top) owns a crocodile farm, Jay Cook (below) runs a Wilderness Camp. – In the Kimberleys cowboys continue work until after nightfall (left). – The Mitchell Falls (large photograph). – Geikie Gorge (top right) is the remains of a coral reef. – Rock paintings tell the mythical stories of the Aborigines (above).

Australia has its "Wild West", too. The highlight of any rodeo, such as this one at Fitzroy Crossing, a town of 1,000 people in the middle of nowhere, is the bull riding. Only the most skillful riders are not thrown off the wildly bucking animals. Not only the rodeo riders themselves and grown up spectators find this event exciting. So do Aboriginal and farmer kids from the neighboring region. They admire the opulent belt buckles and the outfits of the courageous riders. But most of all they admire any attempt to ride the "snorting devils!"

area surrounding the mission in Beagle Bay is under Aboriginal administration and at nearby Cape Leveque the Kooljaman holiday resort is run by the Bardi Aborigines who have sole responsibility over it.

Worlds lie between Cape Leveque and Perth. Western Australia occupies around a third of the entire continent and has an area of 2.5 million square kilometers (965,000 square miles). This is five times the size of Spain. It has 12,500 kilometers (around 7,800 miles) of coastline from north to south. Statistically almost all of its 1.9 million inhabitants live in a single town, in Perth. Located thousands of kilometers from Sydney, this former one-horse town on the west coast was not only one of the most isolated towns in the world for a long time, but also remained rather unknown to most Australians. The urbanites in the large cities in the east used to cast their eye to the dusty west not without a sense of arrogance. This only changed in the 1960s and 70s, when ample mineral resources, such as iron ore, nickel, bauxite, diamonds, oil and gas, were discovered under all the dust. The economic boom which then started attracted mainly young people to the "Australian California" which now overtook Sydney and Brisbane, the Gold Coast and Surfers Paradise. Perth did not only lure people with its affordable real estate and well paid jobs, but also with the most pleasant climate on the continent. Even in winter temperatures rarely drop below 15 degrees Celsius. Surfers have great beaches right on their doorstep and where the new prosperity has formed the skyline of an ultra-modern city, the Swan River meanders right through this metropolis, providing an urban recreation area. Snowy white yachts bob around the jetties of numerous marinas and lend Perth the flair of a "City of Sails". And it also has the flair of a garden city: Perth's King's Park is 4 square kilometers (1.5 square miles) large. Merging with the Botanical Gardens and Langley Park it forms extensive areas of green. Unfortunately, many of the old Victorian buildings were ripped down during the start of the wave of prosperity. Only the pedestrian zone, Hay Street Mall, has retained its atmosphere of colonial times. There are a few architectural pearls left, including Perth's City Railway Station, Town Hall (1867) and The Old Court House (1836). The city of a million, where metropolitan life runs its course remarkably calmly, is not bothered by that. The people of Perth cordially recommend you visit Fremantle, if you like a homogenous old city. Film directors from all around the world have used Fremantle as a colonial backdrop. Perth's port town

was only marked on the world map of tourism when the most spectacular regatta in the world was held there in 1987. Although the Australians lost the much-coveted America's Cup, this event shaped Fremantle into the noble city it is today, with fine restaurants, luxury hotels and numerous galleries.

Colonial flair: the "Exchange Hotel" in the mining town of Kalgoorlie (top). – In the North Hannon Tourist Mine a ranger demonstrates how to get rich with a gold pan (above).

North of Perth the coasts of Western Australia extend up to the Northern Territory, along a length of approximately 3,500 kilometers (2,200 miles). With gorgeous sandy beaches, rugged bays and grandiose river mouths, such as that of Murchison River in Kalbarri National Park, as well as the exotic island worlds of the Buccaneer and Bonaparte Archipelagos. Along the Coastal Highways tourist centers have not only developed in Broome or at legendary Shark

Near Monkey Mia in Shark Bay tame dolphins swim right into shallow water and let themselves be stroked and fed (left). View over the bay of Rottnest Island where many boats are moored (below).

Bay. The bay with the dangerous sounding name was discovered in 1616 by the Dutch seafarer Dirk Hartog, when he happened to sail by. Presumably he was the first European to set foot on Australian territory. Opposite Hartog Island the narrow sand strip attracts tourists, because this is the place where tame dolphins come right up to the shore, allowing themselves to be stroked and hand-fed by the tourists. Thanks to this friendly marine mammal, Shark Bay and Monkey Mia were placed on the World Heritage List in 1991.

While west of Perth the Indian Ocean extends to South Africa, to its east an inhospitable and hot land extends for thousands of kilometers, right to the east coast of the continent. Along the Great Eastern Highway, which only reaches the next Australia city, Adelaide, after 2,000 kilometers (1,240 miles), lie the three gold mining towns Boulder, Coolgardie and Kalgoorlie. For a long time the west was neglected as being uninhabitable, until the gold rush set in and changed this part of Australia into an El Dorado for fortune hunters, adventurers and wheelers and dealers. The splendid Victorian mining towns give you an idea of the incredible values the mining companies dug out from the ground; their mines were amongst the richest in the world at the time. Today, other mineral resources, such as ores, are mined instead of gold. These resources have made Western Australia prosperous.

South of Perth and Fremantle you still have to go a long way to reach the end of Western Australia. If you were to drive right around the coast to the border to South Australia, you would need to be prepared for a distance of 1,500 kilometers (930 miles). But to see the most ravishing beauties of this southwestern tip of the continent, a few hundred kilometers are sufficient. The most beautiful places include the Yalgorop National Park near Bunbury,

amongst the largest on Earth. But apart from mystical cathedral-like chambers, this limestone region has produced another extraordinary thing: "Caves House Hotel" which is over 100 years old and enthroned in the sand dunes of Yallingup Bay, like the set of a Victorian film. In the quiet corners of the coast, contemporary construction culture has secured the loveliest spots for itself. You will come across houses in gorgeous settings, secluded buildings

with an assemblage of idyllic lakes and impressive areas of sand dunes. The temperate climate of the south has supported the development of beautiful cultural landscapes full of contrasts. Grapes out of which the winemakers produce their fine Chardonnays, Sémillons, Sauvignon Blancs and Shirazes grow in the lush green valley of the Margaret River. Connoisseurs find idyllic spots for gentle wine tasting and gourmets find rustically stylish restaurants with high cuisine. Those who like caves can wander through the underground labyrinths of the Mammoth Caves, Lake Caves and Jewel Caves, to name just a few of the most splendid ones. The fantastic stalagmites and stalactites of Jewel Cave are

Shell Beach in Shark Bay is covered with shells (above). The bay is famed for its wealth of fish. But, yes, there are sharks here, too – and not only cute dolphins.

The Australian Pelican is only found in Australia. It has a wingspan of 2.5 meters (8 feet) and more (left).

specimen of the gigantic karri and jarrah trees, whose trunks grow almost as immense as those of the Californian redwoods. These giants, which are up to 400 years old, are the tallest hardwood trees in the world and reach huge dimensions in Pemberton National Park. From these virgin forests of the hinterland, the road meanders back down to the coast. In between gorgeous bays and beaches you will come across place names such as Denmark, Bremer Bay, Ongerup and Bornholm. And in fact they do not only sound Nordic, the area looks it: rolling hills with lush pastures, full of fat grazing cows, seam the coast. Since its foundation as a "timber town" at the end of the 19th century, fishing, vegetable and fruit cultivation as well as animal husbandry has developed in Denmark next to its timber industry. Meanwhile wine is grown here, too, and tourism is

with an architectural design so full of imagination, so very individual. Built of wood, natural stone and glass: you cannot live more beautifully. Near the little picture postcard town Margaret, perfect surf makes this section of the coast a mecca for surfers. The Salomon-Masters competitions which are held here are world class. In adjacent Cape Leeuwin National Park, the cape marks the southwesternmost point of Australia. Pemberton exudes the flair of an old lumberjack settlement. In this region wood is an issue and not only as a raw material. Visitors who did not get weak at the knees and have proven their courage receive a certificate stating: "I climbed the highest fire lookout tree in the world!" The Gloucester Tree. Over 60 meters (200 feet) tall, it is a

growing. The last town on the way to the far east has 30,000 inhabitants and is the oldest town in Western Australia: Albany. It lies between King George Sound and Frenchman Bay and was founded in 1826. It is one of the most picturesque places on the continent. Its houses from the 19th century bear testimony to the past, its surroundings attract nature lovers and hikers with its islands, rocky landscapes and beaches. Whoever comes here will see a picture book landscape – and whales: hundreds of them are sighted in the bays every year. Australia's last whaling station was not only turned into the museum "Whale World", but also into a symbol for peaceful coexistence with the largest marine mammals in the world!

Western Australia is famous for its wealth of wild flowers. Each spring, for a short while, heavy rainfalls transform the outback, the deserts and forests into a sea of colorful blossoms. Banksias, which belong to the family of Proteaceae, are found in bloom throughout the whole state during this time of the year. Banksia (top left and second photograph from below, left column), Swamp Bottlebrush (below right), Acorn Banksia (center, left, right photograph). – The Red-green Kangaroo Paw (top right), too, and the Mottlecah or Silverleaf Eucalyptus create splashes of color.

Holiday dreams come true in Broome: "Camel ride at sunset" on Cable Beach (above) and view of Gantheaume Point (right).

Following double page: Perth's modern skyline developed particularly in the 1980s. From Kings Park you get a good view over the city center. This proud boomtown is surrounded by extensive deserts in the east and by the Indian Ocean in the west.

WAITING FOR THE POSTMAN

THE POSTMEN OF THE OUTBACK

The distances which the postal service of the "red continent" have to overcome are vast. The distance between Perth and Brisbane is 3,606 kilometers (2,240 miles), the dis-

tance from Darwin to Sydney is 3,155 kilometers (1,960 miles). And in between these cities you have got the endless, vast, boiling hot areas of the outback. Here, in the middle of nowhere, there are tiny settlements with just a handful of people as well as individual, isolated sheep and cattle stations. Not always do they have quite the size of Anna Creek Station, which is larger than New Hampshire, USA, with its 24,000 square kilometers (approx. 9,260 square miles). "Connecting Australians wherever they live", is the ambitious motto of Australia Post, even though it is not always easy. Still, the post is always delivered, even to the remotest corner of the continent, for a standard tariff, irrespective of what time and effort

it involves for the postmen and women to get there. The Australian Post makes around five billion deliveries a year, using over 10,000 vehicles. If the delivery areas are extremely

remote from any infrastructure and assuming there is an airstrip nearby, the postman will also take to the air. It should be added that normal airmail has been around for a long time in Australia. Due to progresses that were made in aviation, the first trial run for an airmail service between Melbourne and Sydney was made in 1914. Just a few years later even airmail from England arrived in Darwin. Using the example set by the "Royal Flying Doctor Service", mail runs were set up so that even remote areas could be supplied. For this purpose outback pilots are hired to act as postmen. The most impressive mail run is 2,600 kilometers (1,615 miles) long and reaches from the coast of South Australia far into the out-

back of Queensland. While a normal "postie" has up to 1,200 delivery points on his rounds, the flying postman has not got nearly as many. For instance in Orbost on the coast of Victoria the "flying mailman" sets off every three days for Bonang, on the border to New South Wales, to deliver mail to only one hundred scattered recipients. However, to get to them he has to

Mail delivery at Durham Downs Station (far left): Luke Shields brings the latest news, which is expected with anticipation, to the mail run Port Augusta – Boulder (large photograph and right side, top). – Handing over the mail parcels in Birdsville, Steve in Roseberth is looking forward to mail, Innamincka Station (small photos, clockwise).

and Palmer on the backs of pack horses, there are three mail runs on Cape York Peninsula today. On these mail runs the planes cross the Torres Strait, the Great Barrier Reef, Thursday Island and, naturally, the green rainforests inland. Not all of the Australian mail runs are carried out by airplanes. Twice a week a post bus with a trailer travels across the barren outback, from Coober Pedy to Oodnadatta in South Australia. The bus drives to and fro the same day – a total of 600 kilometers (approx. 370 miles) on bumpy tracks. Right behind Coober Pedy you can see "a lot of nothing", as the Australians like to refer to their motionless inland areas. And in truth there really is not a lot to see, apart from sections of the legendary dingo fence, which the farmers set up over a distance of 5,400 kilometers (about 3,350 miles), to protect their sheep from the Australian wild dogs. This fence is the longest in the world, double the length of the Great Wall of China. After a couple of hours, Anna Creek Station appears on the horizon. Something between 16,000 and 19,000 cattle graze here. Due to the enormous size of the station, the couple of dozen people who work here can only check their herds with the use of helicopters. The next station is William Creek, which claims to be the smallest town in Australia with eight inhabitants and a pub that has

cover a distance of 1,500 kilometers (about 930 miles). In Kununurra, Western Australia, aircraft with mailbags on board take off several times a week to deliver mail to a dozen cattle stations, Aboriginal settlements and tiny villages. In Newman, Pilbara, at the edge of the Great Sandy Desert and the Gibson Desert, twin-engine planes take off regularly on behalf of Australia Post to deliver mail to a handful of families on the stations Turee Creek, Prairie Downs and Tangadee, as well as to the settlements Punmu, Well 33, Cotton Creek, Mount Divide and Balfour Downs near Jigalong in the east. While in 1874 a certain John Hogsfleisch recognized the importance of postal supply and transported mailbags between Cooktown

no competition in a radius of 150 kilometers (around 95 miles). In better days the legendary "Ghan" train of the Central Australian Railway passed by here, on the way from Adelaide to Alice Springs, until the route was moved. The former narrow-gage railway used to be the lifeline of the entire region. The fortune hunters of the mines around Coober Pedy arrived in William Creek by train and then pushed their baggage right across the desert in wheelbarrows to Coober Pedy. Customers sometimes come to the pub, which has managed to keep beer cool since 1887, with their own planes. The thirsty pilots park their aircraft right in front of the pub.

Meanwhile, the comfortably short walk from the pilot's seat to the bar stool was extended for security reasons. Occasionally, so they say, the pilot chose a disconcertingly short braking distance when rolling in.

After a lunch break the post bus sets off again to rumble on to Oodnadatta via Nilpinna, Peake and Allandale Station. Despite modern telecommunication, the postman's visit remains an event for this tiny town of 180 souls. Colorful relicts remain from the era when cattle drivers, Afghan camel drivers, wheelers and dealers and mine workers felt

comfortable here. They include the "Transcontinental Hotel", a few rusty water tanks, the impressive sandstone building of the former train station and The Pink Roadhouse, a pink cross between a grocery store and a truck driver's diner.

The drive back to Coober Pedy takes twelve hours. It is a breakneck drive on unsealed tracks, with dramatic views of surreal desert landscapes and scattered signs of life which really do occasionally exist in Australia's outback. Whoever survives such a trip on a hot summer day won't ever forget boiling heat, a lot of dust and black flies as long as he or she lives and will feel deep admiration for the "Aussies" out there.

"Mailrun by Riverboat" on the Hawkesbury River: the riverboat is used as a post boat (far left). – Passengers on deck (large photo). – Waiting for the mail on the jetty (above right) and hand-over of the mailbags (below).

Those postmen who deliver mail between Port Augusta and Boulia have the most amazing delivery route. They cover a distance of 1,300 kilometers (approx. 800 miles) and complete twenty-five take-offs and landings during their two-day tour. Their prop planes fly along between the Flinders Range and Lake Eyre, across stony Sturt Desert and, on the height of Birdsville, they pass by Ayers Rock approximately 700 kilometers (435 miles) to the east. Beyond the mighty Simpson Desert, the rivers Cooper, Diamantina and Georgina glitter like arteries in the parched landscape in Australia's Channel Country.

In places where the postman enters the wilderness for just 15 minutes, people do not only wait for mail, but especially also for aid and spare parts, without which their survival would be almost impossible. Medical supplies are at the very top of the list. As a consequence the Australian Post and the government have developed a special program where 290,000 delivery points are classified as "remote" to enable a more economical delivery of medical

aid to these places. Educational material is also delivered at a reasonable cost.

Not only those Australian school kids who live on isolated farms and receive their education via Australia's "School of the Air" benefit from this service. A special list compiled by Australia Post, the so called "Remoteness Index", lists places and stations in all Federal States and Territories – between Walgett in New South Wales, Pine Creek in the Northern Territory, Underbool in Victoria, Texas in Queensland, Andamooka in South Australia, Coolgardie in Western Australia and Swansea in Tasmania.

You can book a seat on "the world's longest mail run", as well as on several other Australian mail runs. Almost no outback adventure is comparable to that of the "mail run posties" who not only experience very special geological and geographical views, but who also penetrate deeply into the interior of this rough continent. To the people living there, but particularly also to an important part of its culture and history.

The power of a road train (top), the charm of the desert oasis, Palm Valley (center), the endurance of a camel (below) and the beauty of the birds (right) are just four of the countless things you will experience in the Northern Territory.

NORTHERN TERRITORY

THE RED HEART
THE TROPICAL TOP END
DARWIN

When the sun sets, the heat finally subsides, even in the hot Northern Territory. Now night falls over the country, here in the Rainbow Valley.

You won't get bored in the North. You can watch Australian Rules football (left), go fishing (right), or simply admire the flowers in one of the many national parks (center).

The Northern Territory is part of Australia's vast outback.
And it is certainly the most interesting part, as this is where you will find real natural sensations,
such as Ayers Rock and the Olgas, Kings Canyon and Katherine Gorge,
as well as Kakadu and Litchfield National Park.

Tourists who climb the holy mountain of the Aborigines are called mingas – ants. This is how the indigenous people of Australia refer to these tourists from all over the world, because, seen from the ground, they do look like ants when they crawl up Ayers Rock. This giant monolith 348 meters high (1,141 feet) sticks out from the flat plain and with its circumference of over 10 kilometers (6 miles) it is easily seen from miles away when you approach it on the Lasseter Highway. Earlier you pass Mount Connor which is almost as impressive and which many travelers erroneously assume is the Rock itself.

Ayers Rock is not only located in the middle of the Uluru-Kata Tjuta National Park, but also in the red heart, the geographical center of the "fifth continent". It is a symbol of Australia, just like the kangaroo or the Opera House in Sydney. Consequently the temptation of some to climb it is large. "We don't really like the tourists climbing up our mountain, but we tolerate it", an Anangu ranger, working for the administration of the Uluru-Kata Tjuta National Park, tells us. The tribe of the Anangu has leased the mountain so as not to deprive the tourists of a highlight. For 82 percent of all German tourists, Ayers Rock is the main attraction in the Northern Territory. And Clare Martin, Chief Minister of the Federal State and also Minister for Tourism, naturally wants to keep her approximately 1.7 million visitors per year, of which around 53,000 come from Germany, happy.

So it really is a personal decision whether you choose to climb up Uluru, Ayers Rock in the language of the Aboriginals, and wear the

The heritage of the forefathers, such as the rock paintings at Nourlangie Rock (left page), instills pride and self-confidence in the young generation of Aborigines.

sticker "I climbed Ayers Rock", or not. The alternative thing to do is to walk around this holy mountain of the Aborigines at a respectful distance, admire the cave paintings which are 20,000 to 40,000 years old and then proudly wear the T-Shirt stating: "I didn't climb Ayers Rock". Around 300,000 tourists visit Ayers Rock every year. And each year there are numerous accidents during the ascent or the descent; sometimes these accidents are fatal. Each accident during the climb is also an accident for the Anangu, as they feel responsible for their visitors, being the guardians of this ancient rock. This is one of the reasons why the mountain is off-limits to everyone in the summer, when temperatures rise above 38 degrees Celsius. After all, the climb up and down the mountain takes two to three hours. This is quite strenuous, even in the Australian winter when temperatures drop to a mild 20 degrees out here. The (pointless) up and down record is currently only 24 minutes, believe it or not...

People often think that Ayers Rock and the surrounding National Park is the Northern Territory and the outback. But despite its size, it is only a very small part of it. The Northern Territory is one of the last large nature and wilderness areas on our planet, with unique landscapes, beautiful natural attractions and a diverse fauna. It is covered by tropical vegetation on its north coast and by bush and desert in its center. With an area of 1.35 million square kilometers (521,000 square miles), it is the third largest Federal State of Australia and four times the size of Germany. The MacDonnell Ranges in the south reach a height of 1,500 meters, while Arnhem Land in the north drops down to sea level towards the Arafura Sea. Located in between is the Barkly

Tableland, which is primarily pasture land, the Tanami Desert in the west and the Simpson Desert in the south. These areas are amongst the driest and sandiest on the entire continent. Occasionally camel tours are lead through the Simpson Desert. They leave from Old Andando, six hours drive southeast of Alice Springs. The approximately twenty camels are only employed to carry up to 4 tons of equipment, including provisions and tents,

The Aborigines call the Devil's Marbles, which are found close to Stuart Highway and which were formed by erosion, the "eggs of the rainbow snake". – They are the ideal place for the spinifex pigeon to find shelter.

while up to twelve guests, who are looked after by four guides, set off on the long march through the desert. The trek can be up to 420 kilometers (260 miles) long and take four weeks. The Simpson Desert with its bizarre rock formations and high sand dunes is one of the most interesting, but rarely visited landscapes of the outback.

Just a few decades ago the entire red center was still the most remote and lonely region of Australia. This is why, to this day, you will find the largest classroom in the world here. Due to the immense distances involved, kids can often not get to a school, so they receive their lessons via the radio. Here the doctors fly to

their patients, because they cannot expect the patients to suffer the hardship of an overland trip. Well-off farmers sometimes even visit their neighbors by small aircraft. And the outback cowboys use helicopters to herd their cattle.

Only about 200,000 people, at the most, live in the Northern Territory. Around a quarter of them are Aborigines. The distance between Kulgera on the border to South Australia to the capital Darwin is around 1,700 kilometers (1,050 miles). And there are 900 kilometers (560 miles) between the eastern and western boundaries of the state to Queensland and Western Australia respectively. Nowhere else is the vastness, the fascination of the Australian continent so tangible as here in the red centre. Treeless plains, clumps of spinifex moving in the wind, glaring red earth and the air flimmering in the heat. The Australians describe their outback as "plenty of nothing". But this is where ninety-three different kinds of kangaroos and their relatives hop around and billions of bush flies buzz happily. This is where strange people live in desert towns consisting of three inhabitants and where more than forty Aboriginal

continent. Some Aborigines are very professional as guides for such excursions, whilst others keep well away from tourism. But almost all of them have two names – one reserved for civilization and the other for their native homeland. C.J., Collin John, is one of them: on his own land he is called Gabal, like the tree under which he was born. When, on these bush tucker tours, he shows his territory to the foreigners, C.J. turns into Gabal. He points at

languages are spoken. And of course this is where you will hear the "Aussie" slang, a type of English which has very little to do with Oxford English. Distances of a few hundred miles are considered a short trip. And the twenty-eight rock domes of "Kata Tjuta", as the Olgas are called by the Aborigines, are the only elevation you can see from Ayers Rock. The distance of 43 kilometers (27 miles) seems like a stroll to the next tram stop.

Meanwhile there are numerous tours with Aborigines on offer, during which you learn a lot about distances and boundaries, Dreamtime and songlines, the wilderness with all its animals and plants and the archaic culture of these original inhabitants of the

Both the landscape and the animals of the Northern Territory are bizarre and can sometimes be unfriendly. Chambers Pillar (above) and the dangerous looking, but harmless "Thorny Devil" (left) clearly illustrate this. This species of lizard is common in Uluru National Park.

You can only do this in the Australian winter: cycling, especially with baggage (below), can become torturous in the hot outback. Even the many wild flowers along the way will not be of any consolation then (left).

this and that without saying a word, carefully picks a leaf, rubs it between his fingers, lets people smell and points at his chest: natural medicine described authentically. His tours take several days and these hours of silence, without him uttering a word, tell you a lot about the nature of the Aborigines. Others perform a show, mainly those on the shorter tours. Here Dean loudly warns you about snakes or, with a grin, offers you finger-thick, 10-centimeter long worms from rotten wood as a little snack in between. They are witchetty grubs, which the Aboriginal kids used to have to eat up, like we used to have to eat up our spinach. To make us big and strong.

These "life-in-the-bush tours" are garnished with lessons on reading animal tracks, on hunting techniques, including how to throw a boomerang and a spear and other survival tricks. But nowadays you will also find bush tucker or bush food on some of the menus in towns and cities. It has become popular in the gourmet restaurants of Sydney and Melbourne.

Alice Springs, the only town in the center which comes even close to deserving this name, seems almost like a small metropolis planted into the desert after the outback tours. And Alice, as the Australians call this place, is only a small town with just 25,000 inhabitants. The laying of the telegraph cable from Adelaide to Darwin was responsible for the development of this outback metropolis. And there is a story behind its name. The spring, which was discovered here, guaranteed a regular water supply and was given the name of the wife of the President of the Australian Telegraph Company: Alice. But up until the end of the 1920s, Alice Springs did not even have one hundred inhabitants. No wonder: before the railway line to Adelaide was built in 1929, Alice could only be reached by camel caravans. And only since the beginning of 2004 can visitors travel across the Australian continent from north to south by train. The route of the legendary "Ghan" was only extended to Darwin in the 21st century, although it had been in planning since 1929. Now the train takes just forty-seven hours for the

Unknown water bodies should be avoided, and not only in Litchfield National Park (right). Everything seems fine in Buley Rock Hole (above).

distance of 2,979 kilometers (1,851 miles) from Adelaide to the capital of the Northern Territory. But it would be a shame if this train ride were non-stop. Fortunately you can get off at Port Augusta, Coober Pedy and Alice Springs to have a look around.

The headquarters of the "Royal Flying Doctor Service" and the "School of the Air" are not the only places of interest in Alice. The historic Old Telegraph Station just outside of town is worth a visit, as is the new Aviation Museum, the Spencer and Gillen Museum which shows works of art depicting the natural environment around Alice or the Frontier Camel Farm, which is a short distance out of town, too. You will find even more animals in the Desert Park, a kind of outback zoo where you can see animals which you would not usually come across in the wild. The nocturnal Bilby with its long rabbit ears or the very photogenic Thorny Devil who has a liking for ants. But the new star amongst the animals in Alice is definitely "Terry the Territorian", a large saltwater crocodile which was brought to the Alice Springs Rep-

There are around 500 different species of eucalyptus in Australia. The tallest species can grow up to 90 meters (295 feet) high. – Following double page: termite hills at the break of dawn in Litchfield National Park.

tile Centre by truck from Darwin. Of course Terry has his own enclosure with a nice pool, a shady spot for having a nap and two viewing platforms. One of them enables courageous visitors to look into Terry's green-yellow eyes close up. Terry is the only crocodile in the desert-like outback of the Northern Territory. But most of the other 100 animals in the Reptile Zoo would not be much more than an appetizing starter for Terry.

You get the best view over Alice Springs from Anzac Hill. From here you can also see the Stuart Highway which leads to Adelaide. Only since 1987 has it been sealed all the way. You get to Ayers Rock and the Olgas via the Stuart Highway and the Lasseter Highway. En route you can take a small detour to Rainbow Valley, the Australian equivalent of the American Monument Valley. You can get an idea of the force with which a meteorite can crash onto Earth: the Henbury Crater has a diameter of 180 meters and was created 4,700 years ago when a meteorite came down close to today's Stuart Highway. You can also easily drive to the East MacDonnell Ranges and the spectacular West MacDonnell Ranges from Alice Springs. In the western part of the mountain range you will come across Standley Chasm, Simpsons Gap and Ormiston Gorge. Standley Chasm is amazing. It is only 6 to 9 meters across with steep walls 80 meters high. And finally, on your way from Alice to Kings Canyon, you should not miss out on Finke Gorge National Park with its oasis, Palm Valley, nor on the mission station Hermannsburg, which was founded in 1877. The German ethnologist Albrecht Strehlow looked after Aborigines, who were persecuted at the time, at this station. The church, the school and Strehlow's house from colonial times have all remained unchanged. Here time seems to have stood still...

The next destination is Watarrka National Park, where you will also find Kings Canyon. Hikers have been lost for days in this canyon which seems clearly structured, easy to follow and is 350 million years old. Still, do not allow this to frighten you off. But take a good map and a lot of water along with you. The hike in or around Kings Canyon, a dramatic giant gorge with red rock walls up to 250 meters high in the Ernest Gilles Range, is worth every effort. You will remember your feeling of excitement walking along the steep, unsecured cliffs, the couple of times you might have taken a wrong turn in the labyrinth of the rock domes and the luxurious relaxation in the water-filled pools of dramatic canyons for years to come! Names such as Lost City or Garden of Eden along the Canyon Walk are certainly no fantasy names or exaggerations.

See page 199

A camel safari from Stuart Wells to the Rainbow Valley is not only a lot of fun, but an intense experience. You have to hang on tight when the camel gets up suddenly. It straightens its hind legs first. You sleep in a swag – a canvas bedroll and foam mattress on a frame. Of course you can't do without a romantic camp fire. Even the extremely tough camels need a break in the hot outback. Tourists with no prior experience in riding camels would hardly survive a safari without a saddle (clockwise from top left). The safaris take up to four weeks!

THE GARDEN OF EDEN
KAKADU NATIONAL PARK

Any visitor to the north of the Northern Territory will head towards at least one of its national parks, usually to Kakadu. Some 200,000 visitors come to the Top End every year, mainly to see this UNESCO site of cultural and natural world heritage. Kakadu is around 150 kilometers (approx. 95 miles)

southeast of Darwin and is accessible by a sealed road. It presents an excellent cross section of the regional flora and fauna and you will also find some very well preserved rock paintings of the local Aborigines. Within the park itself you will need a four-wheel drive in parts. It is best to get up-to-date information from the Visitor Centre in Jabiru, including information on the road conditions. During the wet season it is quite possible that you can only guess where the roads are by a sign which might be sticking out from the floods. Still, the park is open throughout the year, as the species' diversity is most visible during the wet season from November to April, during which 90 percent of the rain falls. This is when the vegetation is most lush and countless birds inhabit the wetlands. Anyway, Ubirr and Nourlangie Rock emerge above any flood and so do the famous

Aboriginal paintings on them. From here you get a fabulous view, too. The waterfalls, such as the Jim Jim Falls with its 215 meters (705 feet) in height, simply roar down, due to the huge volumes of water. On a boat trip it is possible to see a crocodile swim by.

With almost 20,000 square kilometers (around 7,700 square miles), Kakadu is the largest national park in Australia. Some say it is the most beautiful one, too. Just like the Uluru-Kata Tjuta National Park in the center of the continent, Kakadu National Park has been

given back to the Aborigines. They, in turn, have leased their land back to the government so that it can be used for tourism and can continue to be used for uranium mining. This is the home of the Gagadju tribe. The name Kakadu was derived from their name and not, as is often wrongly assumed, from the many cockatoos in the park. There are around 300 bird species, 2,000 species of insect, 60 species of mammal, 77 different species of fish and amphibians and 75 species of reptile, including the large saltwater crocodile, water monitors, the long-necked turtle and the frill-necked lizard. On top of that 200 different kinds of ant

the main river channels which are covered by countless plants, including the lotus flower and water lilies, particularly during the wet season. Dense monsoon rainforest and hilly woodlands and the start of the Arnhem Land plateau, an eroded block of sand, the first signs of which stick out of the woodland miles before the actual plateau starts, like islands. Ubirr and Nourlangie Rock are examples of this. Extensive, almost untouched bush and forest landscapes with rivers and ponds, which are called "billabongs" here, give you the feeling of being in the Garden of Eden, endlessly remote from civilization, at least if you leave

ensure busy traffic and sizeable termite hills. Some of the plants and animals in the park have not yet been classified. Many species are endemic, they are only found here.

This natural diversity and the Aboriginal rock paintings, which are up to 23,000 years old, will render your visit to Kakadu a unique experience. Experts divide Kakadu National Park into five zones: the tidal zone including the coast, the river mouths and the mangrove forests with their 22 different mangrove species. The flood plains with the side arms of

the main route a little with your four-wheel drive or on foot. But even on an organized boat trip in the Yellow Waters or on Alligator River you will experience pure idyll – at least until you catch a glimpse of the first large crocodile and pull your arm back into the boat quickly.

A Yellow Water boat trip (left page) guarantees close contact with sea eagles, crocodiles, herons and ibises (from left to right). The view from Ubirr Rock is so beautiful it takes your breath away.

What Alice Spring represents for the center, Darwin represents for the north: the focal point for a whole region. Between these two poles nothing happens along the almost endless Stuart Highway for hundreds of kilometers – or better said: almost nothing. There is Wycliffe Well, the self-appointed world capital of UFO's where extraterrestrials stare at you from the walls of the gas station and UFO's glide around on posters. And there is Tennant Creek, a typical outback town with a little more than 3,000 inhabitants. This is the place from where you set off to have a look at the famous Devils Marbles which have heaped up in a flat landscape and which have been formed by erosion. These round granite rocks have a diameter of up to 6 meters (20 feet) and are the eggs of the rainbow snake, according to Aboriginal mythology. An art and culture center, which gives a clear picture of the history of the Aborigines in this part of Australia, also opened recently in Tennant Creek. The new center, which is called Nyinkka Nyunyu in the language of the Aborigines, is run by the tribe of the Warumungu. They give an introduction to their history and life in the Tennant Creek region and present their arts and crafts. Aside from that, people still dig for gold in Tennant Creek, which lies close to the crossroads leading to the Barkly Highway. The history of the first gold rush comes alive during a visit to the underground mines and the gigantic Gold Stamp Battery which still washes gold out of cracked rock with a lot of noise.

All the way to Darwin there remains only vastness, endlessness, monotonous driving – kilometer after kilometer. This is the country of the cattle stations which are hidden somewhere off the highway in the bush. This monotony is frightening and fascinating at the same time and is only disrupted by Daly Waters, a pub, a gas station and a long history. This is where the airline Quantas filled up its planes on international routes in the 1930s. That is why "Daly Waters Pub" was opened and soon received an alcohol license. Apparently there are some who have heard of this pub, although they have never been to the Northern Territory. Its walls and ceiling are plastered with memorabilia. Bras which were left behind are evidence of female visitors and drunken parties…

Darwin, the capital of the Northern Territory, was founded in 1866 as Palmerston. It was almost completely destroyed in 1942, during World War II, and during various storms, particularly in 1974. But the people at Top End are tough and rebuilt their city again and again. When Palmerston was nominated as the capital of the Northern Territory in 1911, its name was changed to honor

the natural scientist Charles Darwin. Today around 80,000 people live in the largest town in the north of Australia, which has become the gateway to Australia for Asian countries. Meanwhile it is home to people from more than 50 nations and to the Aboriginal Larrakia tribe. Darwin has a tropical climate with high

Yellow Water Lagoon is particularly tranquil in the early evening (left page). – Darwin is the complete opposite with its open-air restaurants (top) and its night market at Mindil Beach (above).

temperatures of between 30 and 35 degrees Celsius throughout the year, high humidity for part of the year and torrential rainfalls during the wet season, which lasts from November to March. Darwin is the sunniest capital on the continent with eight and a half hours of sun a day. But merely Government House, the Court and the ruins of Old Town Hall are worth a visit. The crocodile farms in the wider area are more interesting. As are the many beaches.

Kings Canyon lies in one of the most beautiful national parks of the Northern Territory (left). Hikers also like Finke Gorge National Park, where Mpaara Walk, amongst other hikes, waits for them.

But you should not enter the water during the wet season, as this is when stinging jellyfish swarm in the coastal waters. A vineyard has caused great excitement in this town which loves its beer (the annual consumption of beer per capita is more than 200 liters or 53 gallons): a magnificent wine, made of ripe mangoes, matures in the casks of the Kakadu Winery.

But that is not enough reason for anybody to travel to the north. Everybody just passes through Darwin on their way to the parks of the green, tropical Top End. The number one attraction is Kakadu National Park and Nitmiluk National Park with the canyons of Katherine Gorge and Katherine River. There you can see historical cave paintings of the Jawoyn Aborigines and gorgeous waterfalls.

Near the town of Katherine, a good 300 kilometers (around 185 miles) south of the capital of the Territory, you can visit the friendly Aborigines community Manyallaluk, the Cutta Cutta cave system, the hot springs of Mataranka, the Flora River Nature Park plus Edith Falls.

Litchfield National Park is often referred to as the little brother of Kakadu National Park. And this is despite more places to swim here than in Kakadu. Throughout the year great waterfalls, such as the

artists meet up at the annual "Garma Festival" in Gulkula. One of the loneliest parks, blessed with a lovely coast, is the Keep River National Park in the west. The adventurous can stop off at Gregory National Park, too, which is known for its sandstone gorges, before it's back to Darwin again, where almost all roads lead to.

Florence Falls or the Wangi Falls, pour down from the plateau mountains and fill up pools which are like oases and crocodile free. The second attraction is the termite hills which get up to 6 meters high (200 feet) and which are orientated in a cross-like fashion towards north-south and east-west. You should plan at least a day for Litchfield National Park. For other areas, such as Arnhem Land in the east, you need to plan this amount of time just to get there. A good time of the year to visit Arnhem Land is August when Aboriginal

The rock dome on the canyon plateau of Kings Canyon is one of the most impressive parts of Watarrka National Park. You can spend days wandering through this park, without passing the same spot twice (above).
These wild flowers grow at Chambers Pillar, approximately 100 kilometers (62 miles) south of Alice Springs (left).

201

Katherine Gorge (above) is 12 kilometers (7.5 miles) long and has thirteen side canyons. You will get a proper feel for the dimension of Kata Tjuta – "many heads" in the language of the Aborigines – if you take a flight over the Olgas. There are precisely thirty-six rocky domes (right).

Picture book Australia: the Aborigines have held their clan rituals at Uluru (Ayers Rock) for 10,000 years (following double page).

DREAMTIME AND NOW

AUSTRALIA'S ABORIGINES

The story goes that angry Aborigines shouted "Warra! Warra!" when Captain Arthur Phillip sailed into Port Jackson in 1788 to drop off the first British onto Australian land: "Go away!" Maybe they had an idea of what their fate would be when they saw what kind of people climbed ashore. The majority were prisoners who had been convicted to be deported. At this moment in time this process of civilization could not be stopped anymore. Mythical "Terra Australis", which Cook had reported back to London about enthusiastically, was to be colonized. That had been firmly decided. At the same spot where the Aborigines were threatening with their spears, the Sydney Opera House would be built later on. "All they seem to desire is for us to depart again as soon as possible", Cook noted in his diary following these hostile encounters. But the Aborigines did not have a chance against the incessant stream of immigrants and the fire power of the soldiers. The faster colonization progressed, the more frequent was the contact between the Europeans and those strange dark-skinned people whose mythology of how everything began consisted of Dreamtime spirits, holy mountains and inexplicable energies, of totem beliefs and mysteries. The "civilized" new settlers were confronted with a phenomenon: the "savages" refused all their modern achievements in an almost offensive manner. It was a clash of cultures, as John Turnbull reported in 1805 in his travel report "A Voyage Round the World": "... it is almost the only settlement in the world in which the residence of Europeans has produced absolutely no change in the manners, or useful knowledge of the natives…they have gained nothing in civiliza-

Impressive scenes from the life of the Aborigines: dance performance at the "Barunga Cultural & Sports Festival" (above left and right) and in "Cairns' Tjapukai Aboriginal Cultural Park" (large photograph). Manyallaluk, Aboriginal Cultural Tour: spear demonstration and a South African woman with Aboriginal kids (right page, both pictures top right).

tion since their first discovery. They are still the same savages as in the time of Phillips and their first settlement." Thirty years later the natural scientist Darwin painted a more favorable picture: "In tracking animals or men they show most wonderful sagacity; and I heard of several of their remarks which manifested considerable acuteness. They will not, however, cultivate the ground, or build houses and remain stationary ..." While the Aborigines lost their rights and their land through the progressive colonization, many educated Europeans felt a vocation to find out the reason for this rigorous rejection of western civilization, how to convince them otherwise and to make them in some way useful to society. One of the most striking results of these efforts was when "one of their chiefs, Bennelong, a warrior of great repute, it is said ..." was invited to come to London by the British governor. Turnbull writes: "While Bennelong, the Botany Bay chief was in England, he was presented to many of the principal nobility and first families of the kingdom, and received from many of them presents of clothes and other articles, which a savage of any other country would have deemed almost inestimable. It was not so, however, with Bennelong; he was no sooner re-landed in his own country, than he forgot, or at least laid aside, all the ornaments

and improvements he had reaped from his travels, and returned as if with increased relish, to all his former loathsome and savage habits." Then, Aboriginal children were taken away from their parents and raised in white families. The aim of this experiment was to find out whether the values of civilized culture could be instilled in the savages by upbringing. When they were old enough to decide how to lead their life themselves, they did not hesitate to throw "… aside all their European improvements …" The way the Aborigines were treated during the colonial period demonstrates large cruelty, ignorance and contempt by the Europeans. While the Aborigines in Tasmania were hunted by government proclamation and then interned, countless Aboriginal children were taken away from their clans on the mother continent and put into mission schools. If they did not die of European diseases, most Aboriginal families ended up in reserves. In 1836 Darwin observed "The number of aborigines is rapidly decreasing … This decrease, no doubt, must be partly owing to

the introduction of spirits, to European diseases …and to the gradual extinction of the wild animals." As a consequence, their population shrank to 60,000. Not until 1960 did Aborigines become Australian citizens, with the right to receive social services, two years later were they allowed to vote. Currently, their population is around the same size as during James Cook's time – around half a million. Some things have improved for the Aborigines in the past decades. In 1982 a spectacular verdict by the Australian High Court in the so-called Mabo case accepted land right claims of the Aborigines for the first time. Two years later Werner Herzog's film "Where the Green Ants Dream" was shown in cinemas. In the course of the film a group of Aborigines refuses to leave a narrow strip of land where mineral resources are suspected. They are offered compensation, but they still do not want to move, as they say it is the country where the green ants dream. When one of the mine workers does not want to understand what they are talking about, one of the Aborigines asks him how he would like it if a bulldozer ploughed through his church.

Meanwhile, large areas have been designated as "Aboriginal Land" which is managed by the Aborigines. There are many Federal, semi-Federal and private organizations which provide advice and support to help these people, who have been disadvantaged for so long, to achieve political, economical and social rights. The once so strange seeming culture of the Aborigines has long become part of a new Australian self-concept. Not only in art, but nevertheless particularly in this area: As early as 1904 Leo Frobenius described their "extraordinary skill in drawing and pantomime" in his "Geographische Kulturkunde". Not only expression and painting, but also song and dance played a large role in this society without writing. So it comes as no surprise that art has remained one of their most powerful forms of expression. Their rock drawings, etchings and paintings managed to survive thousands of years. In the meantime, Aboriginal creativity is expressed with acrylics and shown in galleries, museums, on music and theatre stages, in Australian literature and film studios.

Making baskets in Manyallaluk (left page, top); edible seeds (left page, bottom). Digging for roots, bush tucker guide Lorraine (above); Aboriginal women in Barrunga with a work of art (left), rock painting "Wandjina Spirit", King Edward River (large photograph) and Aborigines with kill (around 1873).

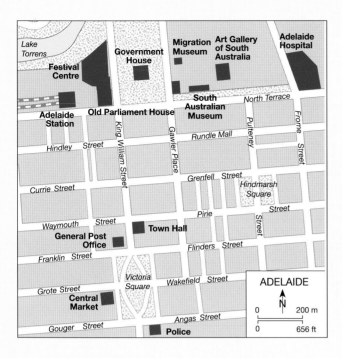

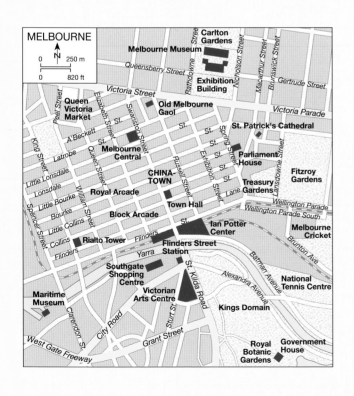

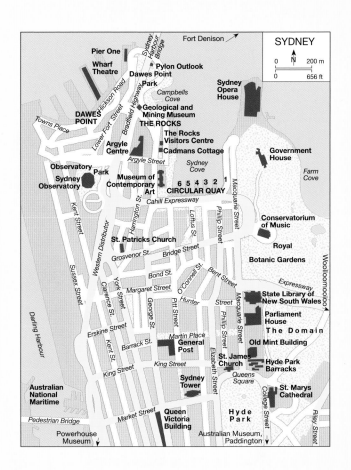
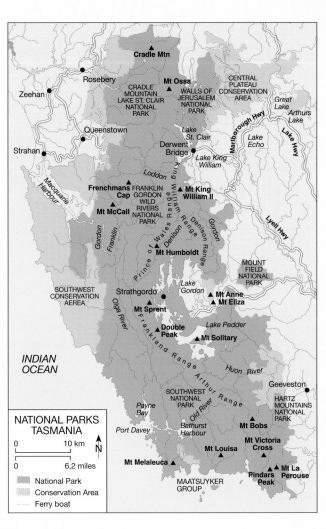

Index

Italic signed pages refer to photos.

People

Aborigines 23, 26, 27, 29, K30, 45, 95, 96, 134, 143, 166, 187, 188, 189, 190, 192, 196, 199, 206, 207, 209
– Anangu 187
– Bradshaw 166
– Gagadju 197
– Jawoyn 201
– Larrakia 200
– Warumungu 199

Bligh William 22

Boston, John 39

Cook, James 22, 45, 50, 56, 73

Dampier William 22
Darwin, Charles 103, 115
Douglas, Malcolm 166

Elizabeth II, Queen 66

Flinders, Matthew 22
Flynn, John 76
Frobenius, Leo 209
Furneaux, Tobias 22

George III 22, 45
Goldsmith, Darilyn 37
Grose, James 67

Hartog, Dirk 22, 170
Hawkins, Jennifer 38
Herzog, Werner 209

Müller, Ferdinand von 82
Murcutt, Glenn 67

Pabst, Johann Christoff 22
Phillip, Arthur (Captain) 22
Popov, Alex 67

Schäffer, Philipp 22
Sears, David 88

Tasman, Abel Janszoon 22, 115
Torres, Luis des 22

Utzon, Jørn 65, 66

Weindorfer, Gustav 117
Welch, Vincent, Dr. 141

Places and things

Adelaide 124, 125, 133, *134, 135,* 171, 191, 212 (map)
Albany 172
Alice Springs *21,* 126, *126/127,* 188, 191, 192
Alpine National Park *80*
Anglesea Barracks 194
Arafura Sea 188
Arnhem Land 188, 192, 197, 201
Atherton Tablelands *2/3, 40, 44, 56, 126*
Australian Open 82, 84
Ayers Rock *4/5,* 26, 27, 127, 187, 192, *204/205*

Ballarat *21, 74, 75,* 82
Barkly Highway 188, 199
Barossa Valley *36/37,* 39, 128, 133
Barramundi *37*
Barunga *185, 206, 208*
Bass Strait 103
Baw Baw National Park 80
Beagle Bay 159
Bedarra 30, 50, 56
Beedelup National Park *154*
Birdsville *17, 18/19, 142, 179*
Blue Mountains 16, *72,* 74, 124

Bonaparte Archipelagos 170
Boulder 171
Boulia 181
"Bounty" 20, *22*
Brisbane 15, 20, *40,* 45, 46, *50*
Broken Hill 76, *89,* 125
Broome 160, *174/175*
Buccaneer Archipelagos 170

Cairns *28,* 29, *31,* 47, *52, 57,* 57, *150/151, 153, 206/207*
Canberra *22/23,* 23, 76
– Capital Hill 76
– National Gallery of Australia 76
– Old Parliament House 76
Cape Leeuwin 172
Cape Leveque 169
Cape Tribulation 29, 58, *60*
Cape York (Peninsula) 22, 57
Carnarvon Gorge National Park *28, 49*
Central Eastern Rainforest Reserve 16
Chambers Pillar 189
Cobourg Peninsula *66/67,* 185
Coober Pedy *137,* 143, *150, 151, 152,* 180, 192
Cooktown 22
Coolgardie 171
Cradle Mountain - Lake St. Clair National Park *28, 102, 110/111, 110, 117, 120/121*
Croajingolong National Park 80
Crocodiles 29, *57,* 58, 166
Curdimurka Outback Ball 145

Daintree National Park *29, 48, 56*
Daintree River 58
Daly Waters (Pub) 199
Dandenong National Park 71, 76
Darwin 20, 127, 188, 191, 199, 200
Dee Why Beach 26
Denmark 172
Derby 140
Devil's Marbles *188*
Dunk Island 30, 50

Eaglehawk Neck 106
East MacDonnell Ranges 192
Eastern Beach 17
Echuca *21*
Eli Creek 16
"Endeavour" 45
Eungelia National Park *60/61*
Eyre Peninsula 134

Family Island 20
Finke Gorge National Park 192, *200*
Fitzroy Crossing *168*
Fitzroy Island *58*
Flinders Chase National Park *28, 128, 131, 132, 133, 137, 145*
Flinders Ranges 136, 181, 143
Flinders Island 106
Flying Foxes 96
Fossil Mammal Sites 16
Franklin-Gordon Wild Rivers National Park 111, 119
Fraser Island 15, 16, 17, 30, *42/43, 46,* 48
Freycinet (Peninsula) 116
Freycinet National Park *98, 101, 110*

Gibson Desert 179
Glenbrook 74
Glenelg 134
Gold Coast *43,* 46, *50, 51*
gold rush 23, 45, 82, 199
Gordon River *118,* 119
Grampians National Park 88
Great Barrier Reef *8,* 16, 17, 27, 29, 45, 52, *52,* 53
Great Dividing Range 150
Great Sandy Desert 179
Great Sandy National Park *46*
Great Wall of China 88, 136
Gregory National Park 201
Gunbarrel Highway *18*

The photographer

Oliver Bolch, born in 1967, graduated from the Master Class of Photography in Vienna. He has been a freelance travel photographer since 1993, his main clients are book and magazine publishers. As a long-term traveler, he gets the opportunity to gain a deeper insight into people and their culture. He won the award for "Best Photography" for his slide presentation "Dream Roads of Australia" at the slide festival El Mundo in 2003. Oliver Bolch is a member of the "Anzenberger Agency". Website: www.oliver-bolch.at
He is also the author of the special "A Piece of the Rainbow – with the Opal Diggers in the Outback".

The authors

Jörg Berghoff, born in 1954, studied History of Art and Ethnology. He is a wine maker and publisher. He is also a freelance author and journalist and has been running a press office since 1988. He travels to Australia regularly and has traveled many other countries, too, as a travel journalist. He is the author of the Chapters "New South Wales and Victoria" and the specials "Food is Served! Excellent wine and multicultural cuisine", "Coat Hangers and Corrugated Iron Roofs – Facets of Australian Architecture", "Melbourne and Its Completely Crazy Horse Race", "Silver Lining on the Horizon – Australia's most Beautiful Train Journeys", "City of Dreams – "Easy Going" in Sydney", and "Wilderness, Vast Landscapes, Adventure – a Trip through the Kimberleys".

Roland F. Karl, born in 1950, is a freelance author and photographer and has been producing travel reports for the printed media for the past 25 years. His contributions have been published, amongst others, in wellknown German newspapers and magazines, for example: "Die Zeit", "Stern", "FAZ", "Frankfurter Rundschau", "Die Welt" and the "Süddeutsche Zeitung". Aside from that, he has contributed to numerous book publications with his texts and photographs. He has traveled Australia several times. The memories of his first trip to the red continent remain particularly vivid: this is when he hitchhiked from Adelaide to Cairns, a distance of 6,000 kilometers (around 3,730 miles).
He is the author of the Chapters "Queensland", "Tasmania", "The North-West" and "Western Australia". Furthermore he wrote the specials "Australia's History", "A World Wonder under Water – The Great Barrier Reef – A Natural Paradise", "On the Trails of the Rangers – Trekking in the Tasmanian Wilderness", "No Distance too Far – the Royal Flying Doctor Service", "Waiting for the Postman – the Postmen of the Outback", "Dreamtime and the Present – Australia's Aborigines".

Jochen Müssig, born in 1959, has been traveling through Australia regularly for the past ten years. He has authored several travel books, published by C.J. Bucher Publishing, and has been working as a travel journalist for the past 25 years. He regularly writes articles for the "Süddeutsche Zeitung", "Die Welt am Sonntag" and has responsibility as chief editor for the renowned "Relais & Châteaux Magazin". He is the author of the Chapters "Take it Easy", "South Australia" and "The Northern Territory" as well as the specials "The Garden of Eden – Kakadu National Park".

Cover photos:

Dust jacket: The "Twelve Apostles" on the Great Ocean Road in Victoria reach a height of 65 meters (213 feet). (Oliver Bolch)

Page 1: "Kata Tjuta" – the Aborigines refer to the Olgas in the red center of the island continent as "many heads". (Oliver Bolch)

Pages 210/211: Aboriginal rock paintings at Ubirr Rock in Kakadu National Park. (Oliver Bolch)

Thanks:

I, Oliver Bolch, would like to thank the following people, institutions and companies for their friendly support during the development of this book:
Werner Claasen – Claasen Communication, Alsbach, Germany; The Mangum Group, Frankfurt, Germany; Text & Aktion, Wiesbaden, Germany; Seven Spirit Bay Wilderness Lodge; Daintree Eco Lodge & Spa; Manyallaluk Aboriginal community; Outback Treasures, White Cliffs; Ocean Spirit Cruises, Cairns – all in Australia; Ruefa Reisen – Austria; Photobörse, Vienna, Austria.

Thank you also to my Australian friends and travel companions without whom many of the photographs could not have been taken: Vida und Adam Takach, Paul Nancarrow; Sonja Krawagner, Jenny Thatcher, Janene Davis, Sonja Tschabuschnig, Christiane Kühling, Brent and Mani Bignell, Family Wharton, Sonja Holocher-Ertl, Heike Ludwig and Helmut Rockstroh, Paul Gloeckl, Michelle Starr and Debra Price.

Special thanks to my parents Ute and Georg Bolch and to Renate Franner, Walter Dunkl and Agnieszka Dukland.

Photo credits:

Archiv für Kunst und Geschichte, Berlin, Germany: p. 22 l. (2)
Artothek, Weilheim, Germany: pp. 24/25
Interfoto, Munich, Germany: p. 23 b.
National State Library of Australia, Canberra, Australia: p. 26 c.
Picture Alliance/dpa, Frankfurt, Germany: p. 22 l (2)
Sotheby's/Archiv für Kunst und Geschichte, Berlin, Germany: p. 26 t.
State Library of Victoria, Melbourne, Australia: p. 209 t.

All other photographs were taken by Oliver Bolch, Maria Enzersdorf, Austria.

We would like to thank all the copyright owners and publishers for their printing permissions. Although we made every effort, we were unable to identify every single one of the copyright owners. We would kindly ask them to contact C.J. Bucher Publishing.

This work has been carefully researched by the author and kept up to date as well as checked by the publisher for coherence. However, the publishing house can assume no liability for the accuracy of the data contained herein.

We are always grateful for suggestions and advice. Please send your comments to:
C.J. Bucher Publishing,
Product Management
Innsbrucker Ring 15
81673 Munich
Germany
E-mail:
editorial@bucher-publishing.com
Homepage:
www.bucher-publishing.com

Translation:
Jenny Baer, Mayerling, Austria
Proof-reading:
Toby Skingsley, Munich, Germany
Series design:
Axel Schenck, Bruckmühl, Germany
Graphic design:
Werner Poll, Munich, Germany, revised by Agnes Meyer-Wilmes, Munich, Germany
Cartography: Astrid Fischer-Leitl, Munich, Germany

Product management for the German edition: Joachim Hellmuth
Product management for the English edition: Dr. Birgit Kneip
Production: Bettina Schippel
Repro: Repro Ludwig, Zell am See, Austria
Printed in Italy by Printer Trento

See our full listing of books at
www.bucher-publishing.com

ISBN 978-3-7658-1625-3